The Rivals

(Modernised English)

Richard Brinsley Sheridan

Re-written for Community Theatre and their Audiences by

Murray Fane

Notes on the Rewrite

I discovered this marvellous play in an old book, covered in dust on a jumble sale table. I was not aware of Richard Brinsley Sheridan but thought the book would pass away some time while on holiday. I read the Rivals and quite simply fell in love with the marvellous humour and warmth of the play.

I spend a lot of my time in community theatre and felt that this wonderful play would have enormous appeal to theatre audiences of the modern era. However, there was one problem. The nature of the old English writing made it very difficult to understand in some places.

So, in a fit of madness, I decided to amend the play to make it more palatable. During the 'modernisation' process I kept the original text whenever I could so that the impact of the original was not lost. However, being an amateur actor, I also tried to ensure it was not a monster to learn.

One of the changes I wrestled with was how to treat Mrs Malaprop's gorgeous errors. In the original, the correct word, and the incorrect word she replaced it with, were frequently obscure. Most of the time I had to reach for the dictionary to find out the meaning of each word. An audience would not have that luxury. So, I had to replace the malapropisms with word combinations that would be readily understood by community theatre goers today. This was without doubt the hardest set of changes to make but I am glad to say that the substitutions did not turn out too bad.

When reading through the play, I was looking forward to the exciting culmination of events at the conclusion. However, I must admit I was a little let down. This is where I took the greatest liberty. I added another duel, which then changed the resolution for Julia and Faulkland. I must admit also that Faulkland annoyed the heck out of me when reading the play, so I took it out on him a bit! Serves him right! I am happy with the way it turned out, and I really hope theatre goers enjoy the change.

Also, in days gone by, it was common to finish with an epilogue. In the original, this perhaps contained the hardest passage to understand. So instead, I took part of the message and wrapped it into a final, much shorter, speech by Lydia.

Finally, a note on the rights to perform this play. My understanding is that the original is open for anyone to perform without royalties. Although I have made many amendments and changed some of the plot, this is still very much Sheriden's play. There may be a charge to perform my version of the play, but it will be very reasonable. The aim is to get the play back on stage rather than retiring as a millionaire.

Contact me on murray.fane@yahoo.com for the rights to perform.

Cast

SIR ANTHONY ABSOLUTE. The Master

CAPTAIN ABSOLUTE. The Young Master. He masquerades as ENSIGN BEVERLEY. In love with LYDIA.

LYDIA LANGUISH. Wealthy young lady. In love with ENSIGN BEVERLEY. Does not know he is CAPTAIN ABSOLUTE. She is JULIA's cousin.

JULIA MELVILLE. LYDIA's cousin and lover of FAULKLAND.

FAULKLAND. Lover of JULIA.

MRS MALAPROP. Tough old aunt to LYDIA

SIR LUCIOUS O'TRIGGER. In a lover's correspondence with MRS MALAPROP, believing her to be LYDIA

ACRES. A suitor for LYDIA. MRS MALAPROP replaces him for the CAPTAIN.

FAG. CAPTAIN ABSOLUTE's man servant

DAVID. SIR ANTHONY's footman. Becomes ACRES' manservant.

LUCY/NARRATOR. LYDIA LANGUISH's maid. Seen as a simpleton, but sharp as a tack.

Scene

Bath

All activity occurs within one day

Act 1

Scene 1

(Outside in the park)

(Each character strolls into view separately, ignoring LUCY)

LUCY: *(In a cockney accent)* Welcome ladies and gentlemen to our tale of love and passion. *(Point to an old couple)* Do you remember love and passion? When you first met your sweetheart – is that your sweetheart there? Do you remember when your tummy fluttered and flipped in apprehension when your lover first came into sight.

Ladies and gentlemen, cast your minds back to those heady days when your eyes met across the crowded room and your heart leapt like a red deer spotted by a poacher. For that is where our young lovers find themselves. Meet the beautiful young heiress, Lydia Languish…

(Enter LYDIA)

LYDIA: Ah my darling Ensign Beverley. He is as poor as I am rich. And though my aunt refuses to allow me to marry him, we will soon elope and live happily ever after in poverty…

(Exit LYDIA, Enter ABSOLUTE)

LUCY: And the object of her love, Ensign Beverley….

ABSOLUTE: Ah my darling Lydia Languish. She loves me as Ensign Beverley and I adore her in return. Yet if she knew the truth, she would not have me. For I am really Captain Jack Absolute, the son of the wealthy Sir Anthony Absolute. I must not let my Lydia find out or she will call off our romance.

4

(Exit ABSOLUTE, Enter JULIA AND FAULKLAND from opposite sides, not seeing each other)

LUCY: And we have another pair of lovers. Miss Julia…

JULIA: My Faulkland. I love him so dearly. I loved him even before we were betrothed by my father. I loved him even before he rescued me from a sinking boat. Yet I cannot convince him of my deep affection. Will he ever propose?

LUCY: And her beloved, Mr Faulkland…

FAULKAND: My darling Julia. I do not deserve her. She says she loves me but can I be sure? Is she just indebted to me? I have not seen her for some time. Has she missed me as much as I have missed her? I am too full of doubts to propose.

LUCY: But let us dally no more. Let us watch our two couples explore their passions and anchor their futures happily ever after. If things go well, we should be out of here for a jug of ale in less than 30 minutes.

All, I believe, is perfect. Nothing can go wrong on such a night as this.

(Exit ALL. Enter DAVID crossing the stage. Enter FAG)

FAG: Hey! David! Wait! David!

DAVID: Upon my word! Mr Fag! Give me your hand, my old fellow-servant.

FAG: David! I'm so glad to see you. You look very hearty. Who would think I would see you taking a walk around Bath!

DAVID: Yes, what a surprise! But we are all here. My master, Sir Anthony Absolute, Madam Julia, everyone.

FAG: Indeed!

DAVID: Sir Anthony felt that another fit of gout was about to visit him so he thought he would give it the slip and whisked us all away to Bath with only an hour's warning.

FAG: That's Sir Anthony Absolute for you. Hasty in everything!

DAVID: But tell me Mr Fag, how is the young Master, Captain Absolute? Sir Anthony will get such a shock to see the captain here.

FAG: I do not serve Captain Absolute now.

DAVID: Surely you have not left him!

FAG: At present I am employed by Ensign Beverley.

DAVID: Oh, Mr Fag. An Ensign is the lowest rank possible. I don't think that is a change for the better.

FAG: I haven't changed, David.

DAVID: Didn't you just say you have left the young Master.

FAG: Yes, I have. Ha ha. I'll puzzle you no longer David. Captain Absolute and Ensign Beverley are one and the same person. Currently he is pretending to be the ensign, so that is who I currently serve.

DAVID: What! I am completely lost!

FAG: Can you keep a secret, David?

DAVID: I can be as dumb as a coach horse.

FAG: The cause of this is love David, love. Which has been the source of masquerades since the start of time.

DAVID: Yes, I guessed there was a lady in the picture. But why does your master pose only as an ensign? Now if he had chosen to be a general…

FAG: Ah David. There lies the mystery of the matter. My master, Captain Absolute, is in love with a lady with a very peculiar taste. A lady who likes him better as a poor ensign than if she knew he was son and heir to Sir Anthony Absolute, a baronet of three thousand a year!

DAVID: That is an odd taste indeed! But tell me, how is *she* placed? Is she rich, eh?

FAG: Rich! Why she could pay the national debt as easily as I pay my washerwoman. She has a lap dog that eats out of a gold bowl and she feeds her parrot with pearls.

DAVID: Goodness gracious! Bravo to the young Master! May one hear her name?

FAG: Miss Lydia Languish. But he cannot woo her as freely as he wishes because there is a tough old aunt in the way, by the name of Mrs Malaprop. So they correspond secretly.

DAVID: Well, Mr Fag, I wish them luck and hope it ends in happiness.

FAG: Indeed. Now David did you know Mr Faulkland is also in Bath. We should meet up with his manservant for a little party.

DAVID: A fine idea! I hear Mr Faulkland is to marry a young lady.

FAG: Ah yes, Madam Julia. And that brings things full circle, for Madam Julia and Miss Lydia Languish are cousins.

DAVID: We live in a small world Mr Fag.

FAG: Indeed we do. *(Suddenly seeing the Captain across the street).* But wait David – look, look there! I believe there is the captain.

DAVID: Oh yes! It *is* Captain Absolute, or should I say Ensign Beverley at the moment? Is that the lady with him?

FAG: No, no! That is Madam Lucy, Miss Lydia Languish's maid. I must go and tell him you are all here.

DAVID: Odd! The young Master is giving the maid money....

FAG: Indeed. Money for messages. Their secret love messages are carried by the maid Lucy. Lucy only knows him as Ensign Beverley, she has no idea he is really Captain Absolute.

DAVID: Quite so! Well Mr Fag, I must be on my way.

FAG: And I too. Until tonight, David.

(They both leave)

Scene 2

(Enter LUCY)

LUCY: What a bunch of foozlers. So now you know my role in this tale. I am the bringer of love messages between Ensign Beverley and my lady Lydia. But I must introduce some more people to you...

(Enter MRS MALAPROP and SIR LUSCIOUS separately)

This grand lady is Mrs Malaprop. She is Lydia's aunt and until Lydia is of age, this forbidding aunt controls who Lydia can or cannot marry. Astonishingly, Mrs Malaprop herself has fallen for an Irish baronet by the name of Sir Luscious; a fine-looking man. They correspond only through letters that I bring. But there is a hidden tale there that shall become clear.

(Exit MRS MALAPROP and SIR LUSCIOUS. Enter SIR ANTHONY arm in arm with JULIA)

Aha, here comes Captain Absolute's father Sir Anthony. Sir Anthony is also Julia's guardian. Sir Anthony is an important influential man and I have high hopes he may resolve some of the lover's troubles.

(The tea rooms. LYDIA sitting on a chair with a book in her hand. LUCY, has just returned after LYDIA sent her off on an errand to find a book)

LUCY: Indeed, Miss Lydia. I searched half the town for the book. I don't believe there's a library in Bath I have not visited.

LYDIA: And you could not get *"The Reward of Constancy"* Lucy?

LUCY: No indeed, ma'am.

LYDIA: Nor *"The Mistakes of the Heart"*?

LUCY: As bad luck would have it, the last one at Lewis Bull's shop had just been taken.

LYDIA: Hey-ho. Did you ask for *"The Delicate Distress"*?

LUCY: Yes indeed ma'am. I asked everywhere for it, and I might have brought it from Mr Frederick's Books, but Lady Slattern Lounger had so soiled and dog-eared it, that it wasn't fit for a Christian to read. But here ma'am. *(Taking a book from under her cloak)*. Here are the *"Memoirs of Lady Quality, written by herself"*.

LYDIA: Very good – now pass me the sal volatile.

LUCY: You didn't ask me to get that one ma'am.

LYDIA: My smelling salts, you simpleton!

LUCY: Oh the drops! *(Voices outside)* Here ma'am.

LYDIA: Wait! Surely I heard my cousin Julia's voice, *(Lucy looks through a window)*.

LUCY: Lud, Ma'am! Yes indeed, Miss Julia is here.

LYDIA: Is it possible!

(Enter JULIA, Exit LUCY)

LYDIA: My dearest cousin Julia. How delighted I am. *(Embrace)* How unexpected is this happiness!

JULIA: Indeed, Lydia. I am so full of joy to meet you here. I had not been able to see you in London and I know you have been vexed.

LYDIA: Ah Julia! I have a thousand things to tell you! But first tell me, why are you in Bath? Is your guardian, Sir Anthony Absolute, here?

JULIA: He is. We arrived an hour ago. I am sure he will come soon to meet your aunt, Mrs Malaprop, after he has dressed.

LYDIA: Then before we are interrupted, let me tell you of my distress! I know your gentle nature will sympathise with me. My letters have informed you of my connection with Ensign Beverley. But Julia, I have lost him! My aunt has discovered our relationship through a note she intercepted, and she has confined me to the house.

JULIA: Oh no!

LYDIA: And yet would you believe it; my aunt has fallen in love with a tall Irish baronet she met some nights ago at Lady MacShuffle's social gathering.

JULIA: You jest, Lydia!

LYDIA: No, upon my word. She is corresponding with him daily, although she is using a fictitious name, Delia.

JULIA: Then surely she is now more forgiving to her niece.

LYDIA: On the contrary. Since she has discovered her own weakness, she has become more suspicious of mine. But I must also inform you of another plague. That odious Acres is to be in Bath today. As you know, my aunt has selected him as my suitor, so that will dampen all my spirits!

JULIA: Come, come Lydia. Hope for the best. I believe Sir Anthony is not impressed with Mr Acres and may exert an influence.

LYDIA: Let's hope so. But you have not heard the worst. Unfortunately, I quarrelled with my poor Beverley, just before my aunt made the discovery. I have not seen him since to make up.

JULIA: What was his offence?

LYDIA: Nothing at all! The trouble is, as often as we had been together, we never had a quarrel! Honestly, I was afraid he would never give me an opportunity. Can you believe it! So last Thursday, I wrote a letter to myself, to inform myself that Beverley was at that time courting another woman. I signed it *"your Friend unknown"*, showed it to

Beverley, charged him with being unfaithful, put myself in a violent passion and vowed I'd never see him again.

JULIA: You let him leave and have not seen him since?

LYDIA: The very next day my aunt found us out. I intended to only tease him for three and a half days, and now I have lost him forever.

JULIA: If he is as deserving as you say then he will never give you up. But think seriously Lydia. You tell me he is only an ensign, and you have thirty thousand pounds!

LYDIA: But you know until I am of age, I lose most of my fortune if I marry without my aunt's consent. Well so be it. I will not let others dictate conditions of love to me. So, marrying without consent is what I have determined to do ever since I learned of that pernicious penalty. And therefore, I must love a handsome, but poor man who loves me for myself and not my fortune.

JULIA: Really Lydia! That is such a ridiculous, fanciful whim.

LYDIA: Julia, why do you accuse me of fanciful whims when you are *still* waiting for your lover Faulkland to propose.

JULIA: I admit Faulkland has his faults, but at least he is my equal and has the consent of my family.

LYDIA: Tosh! Have you sent for him to join you here?

JULIA: Not yet. He doesn't even know I am in Bath. Sir Anthony's decision to come was so sudden that I could not inform him of it.

LYDIA: Julia, for a whole year you have been slave to the whims and jealousy of this ungrateful Faulkland. He continues to withhold any marriage proposal while you suffer him to be a haughty and condescending lover.

JULIA: No, you are wrong entirely. We were promised to each other before my father's death. I know marriage is Faulkland's ardent wish. And as for his character, you wrong him there too. No, he is too noble to be jealous. If he criticises, he does so honestly. If he is irritable, he is never rude.

LYDIA: But as a lover?

JULIA: Poor Faulkland, being unused to relationships, he expects every thought and emotion of his mistress to move in unison with his. But his humility means he does not feel deserved to be loved, so he in turn suspects that he is not loved enough. This I must admit has cost me many unhappy hours.

LYDIA: But tell me honestly Julia. If he had never saved your life, do you think you would have been as attached to him as you are? Believe me, the great blast of air that overturned your boat sent a whirlwind of good fortune to him.

JULIA: Gratitude may have strengthened my attachment to Mr Faulkland, but I loved him before he saved me. But even so, in saving me, isn't that enough cause for a binding obligation?

LYDIA: Obligation! Why a water-spaniel would have done as much! I should never think of giving my heart to a man because he could swim!

JULIA: Come, Lydia, you are too inconsiderate.

LYDIA: Nay, Julia, I am jesting.

(Enter LUCY)

LUCY: Oh Lord ma'am. Sir Anthony and Mrs Malaprop are both coming here!

JULIA: I must go. I'll pay my respects to your aunt, Mrs Malaprop another time, when she can treat me to her version of words so ingeniously misapplied without being mispronounced!

LYDIA: Well, I won't detain you cousin. Adieu my dear Julia. I'm sure you are in a hurry to send a message to Faulkland. *(Points)* Go there to find a way out.

JULIA: Adieu! *(Embrace. Exit JULIA)*

LYDIA: Here my dear Lucy. Quick, quick. Fling *Peregrine Pickle* in your coat and leave *Fordyce's Sermons* open on the table.

LUCY: O burn it, ma'am, the hairdresser has torn the pages away as far as 'Proper pride'.

LYDIA: Never mind – open at 'Sobriety'. Now we are ready for them.

(Exit LUCY. Enter MRS MALAPROP and SIR ANTHONY ABSOLUTE)

MRS MALAPROP: There, Sir Anthony, there sits the simpleton who wants to disgrace her family and lavish herself on a fellow not worth a shilling.

LYDIA: I thought *you* once …

MRS MALAPROP: You thought miss! I don't know any business you have to think at all. Thought does not become a young woman. Now, we have come to hear your promise to *forget* this fellow Beverley – to illiterate him from your memory.

LYDIA: Ah, Madam! Our memories are independent of our wills. It is not easy to forget.

MRS MALAPROP: But I say it *is* miss. There is nothing on earth so easy as to forget. I'm sure I have completely forgotten your poor dear uncle as if he never existed. And let me tell you, Lydia, your rampant memories don't become a young woman.

SIR ANTHONY: Why is she remembering what she has been ordered not to. Aye, this comes from her reading!

LYDIA: What crime, madam, have I committed to be treated thus?

MRS MALAPROP: Now don't attempt to explicate yourself from the matter. You know I have inhospitable proof of your dalliance with this ensign. Tell me you will promise to do as you are ordered. Will you take Acres, the husband we have chosen for you?

LYDIA: Madam, I must tell you plainly that I have my preference, and the choice you make would be my aversion.

MRS MALAPROP: What business do you have, miss, with *preference* and *aversion*? They don't become a young woman. You should know

13

that both of these wear off. It is the safest thing in matrimony to begin with a little aversion. I am sure I hated your dear uncle before marriage, and yet you know what a marvellous wife I made. And when it pleased Heaven to release me from him, nobody knows the tears I shed, shortly before I put him out of my memory. But suppose we gave you a choice other than Acres, will you promise us to give up this Beverley?

LYDIA: If I could so easily contradict my thoughts, then, if I give that promise, I am certain my actions would just as easily contradict my words.

MRS MALAPROP: Go back to our lodgings. You are fit company for nothing but your own disagreeable temper.

LYDIA: Willingly ma'am – I cannot change for the worse.

(Exit LYDIA)

SIR ANTHONY: This is not surprising ma'am – all this is the natural consequence of teaching girls to read. If I had a thousand daughters, by heaven I would sooner have taught them black magic than the alphabet!

MRS MALAPROP: Nay nay Sir Anthony, you cannot mean it. You are surely being numerous.

SIR ANTHONY: Am I? On my way here, Mrs Malaprop, I observed your niece's maid coming from a circulating library with a book in each hand! I guessed then that her mistress would have no sense of duty. A circulating library in a town is like an ever-green tree with leaves of lewdness. It blossoms throughout the year. Depend on it, Mrs Malaprop. Those who are so fond of handling the leaves will eventually long for the fruit.

MRS MALAPROP: Tush, tush Sir Anthony. You cannot be serious.

SIR ANTHONY: Well then Mrs Malaprop, what would you have a woman know?

MRS MALAPROP: Sir Anthony, I would not want a daughter of mine to be an apology of learning. I would never let her meddle with Greek, or Algebra, or Ecstatics. I would send her at nine years old to a boarding school to learn a little ingenuity and artifice. Then sir, she should have a supercilious knowledge of accounts. Above all, Sir Anthony, she

14

would be a mistress of orthography, that she might not misspell and mispronounce words so shamefully as girls usually do. And likewise, she may reprehend the true meaning of what she is saying. This, Sir Anthony, is what I would have a woman know; and I don't think there is a superstitious article in it.

SIR ANTHONY: Well, well, Mrs Malaprop. I see you are set and will dispute the point no further with you. So, ma'am let's get to the more important point of our debate. You say you have no objection to my proposal concerning my son Jack.

MRS MALAPROP: None, I assure you. There is no formal engagement with Mr Acres, and as Lydia is so obstinately against him, your son may have better success.

SIR ANTHONY: Good! I will write for the boy to come directly. He does not know anything of this yet and is at present with his regiment.

MRS MALAPROP: We have never seen Captain Absolute, Sir Anthony, but I hope there will be no objection on his side.

SIR ANTHONY: Objection! Let him object if he dare! No, no Mrs Malaprop, Jack knows that any resistance puts me straight into a frenzy. My process was always very simple. In their younger days it was "Jack do this". If he objected – I knocked him down – and if he grumbled at that, I sent him out of the room.

MRS MALAPROP: Indeed, nothing is so disinfecting to young people as severity. Well, Sir Anthony, I shall decease Mr Acres and prepare Lydia to receive your son's infestations. And I hope you will describe her to the Captain as an object not entirely illegible.

SIR ANTHONY: I will madam. Well, I must leave you. But let me beg *you*, Mrs Malaprop, to enforce this matter strongly with the girl. Take my advice, keep a tight hand. If she rejects this proposal, clap her under lock and key. And if you were just to let the servants forget to bring her dinner for three or four days, you can't conceive how she would change her mind!

(Exit SIR ANTHONY)

15

MRS MALAPROP: Well, at any rate I shall be glad to get her from under my intuition. She has somehow discovered my partiality for my Irishman, Sir Lucious O'Trigger. I am sure Lucy could not have betrayed me. No, the girl is such a simpleton, she would have confessed it. Had she been inelegant I should never have trusted her. *(Looking out the window)* Ah there is the silly girl. *(Calls)* Lucy, Lucy!

(Enter LUCY)

LUCY: Good mornin' ma'am.

MRS MALAPROP: Good morning, Lucy. Did you see Sir Lucious while you were out?

LUCY: No, indeed ma'am, not a glimpse of him.

MRS MALAPROP: Lucy, are you sure you have never mentioned my relationship to your …

LUCY: Oh Gemini! I'd sooner cut my tongue out!

MRS MALAPROP: Well don't let your simplicity be imposed on.

LUCY: No ma'am.

MRS MALAPROP: Come to me shortly and I'll give you another letter to Sir Lucious. But mind Lucy – if you ever betray what you are entrusted with (unless it is other people's secrets to me) you shall forever forfeit my malevolence. Though you are but a simpleton I shall still expect your defiance.

(Exit MRS MALAPROP. Lucy talks to herself and not the audience – she is not the narrator at this stage)

LUCY: Ha ha ha! So my dear *simplicity* let me give you a break from this unpleasant pretence. *(Altering her manner to portray an intelligent person)* Let girls in my station keep their cleverness hidden from their mistresses. And under a mask of silliness let their sharp eyes keep on the lookout for their own interests. Let me see how my *simplicity* has increased my account. *(Looking at a paper).* For abetting Miss Lydia Languish in her quest to run away with Ensign Beverley, in money - twelve pounds twelve shillings. Gowns – five, hats, ruffles, caps etc etc – numberless! From the said Ensign, within this month - six guineas and a half – about a quarter's pay! Item *from Mrs Malaprop for betraying the young people to her* – but only when I found matters were likely to be discovered – *two guineas and a black silk gown.* Item, *From Mr Acres, for carrying various letters to Miss Lydia* – which I never delivered – *two guineas and a pair of buckles.* Item *from Sir Lucious O'Trigger – three crowns – two gold pocket charms – and a silver snuff box!* Well done, *Simplicity!*

(LUCY moves position to address the audience and becomes the narrator.)

(Maintaining her intelligent voice) And so you now know my secret; by playing a simpleton I become wealthy through each exchange. A girl has to make a living! So where are we?

(Enter ACRES)

We have a new lover to contend with. Mr Bob Acres was betrothed to Lydia but has been cast aside for Captain Absolute by Mrs Malaprop and Sir Anthony. Mr Acres has no idea at this stage that he has been usurped. What's more Acres is a good friend of Captain Absolute who also has no idea of his proposed match.

ACRES: *(Looking at his watch)* Odds, rockets and racehorses, I have made excellent time. I'll tidy myself up a bit and then call on Mrs

Malaprop and my lovely lady Lydia. Oh, how pleased she will be to see me. Then I will meet my great friend Captain Absolute for a party, for I hear he is also in Bath.

(Exit ACRES, Enter LYDIA)

LUCY: Miss Lydia meanwhile has been told the news that Acres has been replaced by another unwanted suitor, Captain Absolute. I myself have never met this Captain Absolute and I hope my dear Ensign Beverley moves quickly to avoid the loss of his love to this new rival.

LYDIA: I rejoice at the dismissal of Mr Acres but now have to contend with another bore. He may be a captain but will never stand up to my ensign. If only I had not quarrelled with my beloved Beverley. Will I ever see him again?

(Exit LYDIA. Enter SIR LUSCIOUS who gives LUCY a letter then leaves)

LUCY: I have a little confession. You know that Mrs Malaprop is besotted with Sir Luscious, and they pay me handsomely to write lovingly to each other. And to keep the affair a secret in case letters are intercepted she signs herself Delia. My confession is that I was forced to make my Irishman, Sir Lucious, believe that he was corresponding not with the aunt but with the niece, Miss Lydia. For although he is not rich, and Mrs Malaprop is exceedingly affluent, he has too much pride and fragility to pursue his feelings with a formidable aunt just to get hold of her fortune. The niece was a more enticing masquerade to keep the correspondence, and my income, flowing.

(Exit LUCY)

Act 2

Scene 1

(The CAPTAIN and FAG come into the tea rooms)

FAG: Captain Absolute sir, while I was there, Sir Anthony came in. I told him you had sent me to inquire after his health, and to know if you could see him.

ABSOLUTE: And what did he say, Fag, on hearing I was in Bath.

FAG: Sir, in my life, I never saw an elderly gentleman more astonished! He stepped back two or three paces, rapped out a dozen oaths, and asked what the devil brought you here!

ABSOLUTE: Well sir, what did you say?

FAG: Oh, I lied sir – I forget the precise lie, but you may depend on it he got no truth from me. Yet for fear of making a blunder in the future, I should be glad to know what I should say *has* brought us to Bath. Sir Anthony's servants were curious, sir, very curious indeed.

ABSOLUTE: You said nothing to them?

FAG: Oh, not a word sir – not a word. Mr David, his footman, who I take to be exceedingly discrete …

ABSOLUTE: You rascal! You have not trusted him!

FAG: Oh, *no*, sir – no – no – not a syllable. On my word! He was, indeed, a little inquisitive; but I was sly sir – devilishly sly. My master (said I) *honestly* David (you know sir, one says *honestly* to one's inferiors) has come to Bath to *recruit*. Yes sir, I said *recruit*. I did not say what you were recruiting for that is none of his business.

ABSOLUTE: Well, let it be *recruiting* then.

FAG: Indeed sir. And to give the thing some legitimacy, I told David that your honour had already listed five disbanded sedan chair carriers, seven part-time waiters and thirteen billiard score keepers.

ABSOLUTE: You blockhead. Never say more than necessary.

FAG: I beg your pardon sir. But with respect, a lie is nothing unless one supports it. Sir, whenever I invent a good lie, I always dream up a fine back story.

ABSOLUTE: Well, take care you don't hurt your credit by offering too much security. Now, is Mr Faulkland coming here?

FAG: He will be here any minute, sir.

ABSOLUTE: Do you know if he has been informed of Sir Anthony's and Miss Julia Melville's arrival?

FAG: I believe not, sir.

ABSOLUTE: Good. That is all Fag.

FAG: Yes sir *(Going)*. I beg your pardon sir but if you see Sir Anthony, will you do me the favour to remember that we were *recruiting*, if you please.

ABSOLUTE: Yes, yes.

FAG: And I would be much obliged to you sir if you would bring in the sedan chair carriers and waiters. For though I would never hesitate to invent a lie to serve my master, it does hurt one's conscience to be found out. *(Exit FAG)*

ABSOLUTE: Now for my whimsical friend – since he does not know that his mistress Julia is here, I'll tease him a little before I tell him.

(Enter FAULKLAND).

Faulkland, so good to see you in Bath again.

FAUKLAND: Ah my fine friend Captain Absolute! Well Jack, what is the news since I left you? How are things with you and Lydia?

ABSOLUTE: Faith, they are much as they were. I have not seen her since our quarrel.

FAUKLAND: Why don't you find her and persuade her to go off with you at once?

ABSOLUTE: What and lose two thirds of her fortune? Don't forget that my friend. No, I could have persuaded her long ago.

FAUKLAND: My friend, your time wasting has gone on too long. If you are sure of her then write to her aunt as your true self and then write to Sir Anthony for his consent.

ABSOLUTE: No, I must tread carefully. Though I am convinced my little Lydia would elope with me as Ensign Beverley, I am by no means certain that she would take my wealthy other self. No, no I must prepare her gradually for the discovery, and make myself irresistible to her before I risk it. Well now Faulkland, will you dine with us today at the Assembly Rooms?

FAULKLAND: *(Morosely)* Unfortunately I cannot. I am not in good spirits for such a party.

ABSOLUTE: Good heavens Faulkland! You don't want my company! I swear when you are in love you are a stubborn, frustrating man!

FAULKLAND: I admit I am unfit for company.

ABSOLUTE: Am *I* not a lover? And do I carry around with me such a confounded mess of doubts and fears like a featherbrained numskull?

FAULKLAND: Ah Jack. Your heart is not like mine, fixed constantly on only one object. You play hard to win a lady's hand, but if you lose then you find another game. But I have set my heart on the one and only Miss Julia.

ABSOLUTE: For heaven's sake! You and Julia are a fine match. What has your whimsical brain conjured up now to leave you in such a miserable mood.

FAULKLAND: Heavens there are a thousand reasons! I fear for her spirits, her health, her life. She'll be upset and anxious waiting for my return. If it rains, some shower may have chilled her delicate frame. If the wind blows strongly, some rude blast may have affected her! Oh Jack when delicate and feeling souls are separated, every movement of the elements hints that some terrible misfortune will come her way.

ABSOLUTE: But we can choose whether we take the hint or not. So Faulkland, if you could be convinced that Julia was well and in good spirits, would you be entirely content?

FAULKLAND: I should be happy beyond measure.

ABSOLUTE: Then to bring you delight at once – Miss Melville is in perfect health and is at this moment in Bath.

FAULKLAND: No, Jack, don't trifle with me.

ABSOLUTE: She arrived here with my father less than an hour ago.

FAULKLAND: Are you serious?

ABSOLUTE: Seriously, on my honour, she is here.

FAULKLAND: My dear friend! What joy! Upon my hat – my dear Jack, now nothing on earth can give me a moment's uneasiness.

(Enter FAG)

FAG: I found Mr Acres taking the air, sir. I told him you were here in the tea rooms.

FAULKLAND: I should go.

ABSOLUTE: Stay, Faulkland. Mr Acres lives within a mile of Sir Anthony, and he will tell you how your mistress has been since you left.

FAULKLAND: What, is he well acquainted with the family?

ABSOLUTE: Oh yes, very intimate. I insist on you not going. Besides he is an entertaining character.

FAULKLAND: Good. I *should* like to ask him a few questions.

ABSOLUTE. Faulkland, before he comes in, I must tell you that Mr Acres is a rival of mine – that is of Beverley, my other self. He does not think that his friend Captain Absolute has ever seen the Lady Lydia.

FAULKLAND: Hush! He is here.

(Enter ACRES)

ACRES: Ha ha my dear friend, noble Captain and honest Jack. How are you? Odds, whips and wheels I have travelled here like a comet, with a tail of dust all the way as long as the Mall.

ABSOLUTE: Ah Bob, you are indeed an eccentric planet. Let me introduce Mr Faulkland to you. Mr Faulkland, Mr Acres.

ACRES: Sir. I am most heartily glad to see you. Hey Jack, is this the Mr Faulkland who –

ABSOLUTE: Indeed yes Bob, Miss Julia Melville's Mr Faulkland.

ACRES: Well I never! She arrived with your father just before me. I suppose you have seen them already. Ah! Mr Faulkland you must indeed be a happy man.

FAULKLAND: I have not seen Miss Melville yet sir – I hope she enjoyed good health and spirits when in Devonshire?

ACRES: Never knew her better in my life sir – never better. Odds, blushes and blooms! She has been as healthy as a thermal spa.

FAULKLAND: Indeed! – *(hopefully)* I heard that she had been a little indisposed.

ACRES: False, false sir. That must have been said only to distress you. Quite the reverse I assure you.

FAULKLAND: There, Jack. You see she has an advantage over me. She is fine while I had almost fretted myself sick.

ABSOLUTE: Now you are angry with your mistress for not having been ill!

FAULKLAND: No no, you misunderstand me. Yet surely a little trifling indisposition is not unnatural when absent from those we love. Isn't there something unkind in this rampant, unfeeling health, Jack?

ABSOLUTE: Oh, it was very unkind of her to be well in your absence to be sure!

ACRES: *(Laughing)* Well said Jack!

FAULKLAND: Well sir, you were saying that Miss Melville has been so *exceedingly* well. I suppose she has been merry and gay, hey?

ACRES: Merry, odds and crickets! She has been the belle of the ball wherever she has been – so lively and entertaining! So full of wit and humour!

FAULKLAND: There, Jack, there. Oh, by my soul, there is an innate levity in the woman that nothing can overcome. What! She is *happy* while I am away!

ABSOLUTE: Hush Faulkland – how foolish is this! Just a few minutes ago, you said you would be happy beyond measure if she was well and in good spirits!

FAULKLAND: Why Jack, have *I* been the joy and spirit of the company?

ABSOLUTE: No indeed, you have not.

FAULKLAND: Have *I* been lively and entertaining?

ABSOLUTE: Upon my word I cannot accuse you of that.

FAULKLAND: Have *I* been full of wit and humour?

ABSOLUTE: No, faith! To do you justice, you have been confoundedly stupid indeed.

ACRES: What's the matter with the gentleman?

ABSOLUTE: He is only expressing his great satisfaction at hearing that Julia has been so well and happy – hey Faulkland?

FAULKLAND: *(Happy)* Oh, I am rejoiced to hear it. Yes, yes, I am pleased that she has a happy disposition!

ACRES: That she has indeed – then she is so accomplished – so sweet a voice – so expert at her harpsichord. Earlier in the month, odds, minims and crotchets, how she did chirrup like a nightingale at Mrs Piano's concert.

FAULKLAND: There again! What do you say to this Absolute! You see, she has been laughter and song all along – not a thought of me!

ABSOLUTE: Nonsense man! Is not music the food of love?

FAULKLAND: Well, well, it may be so. Pray Mr – what's his damned name? Do you remember what songs Miss Melville sang?

ACRES: I am afraid I do not.

ABSOLUTE: Mr Acres. I am sure there were some sorrowful, melancholy and grim tunes. Perhaps you may remember – did she sing 'When absent from my soul's delight'?

ACRES: No that wasn't it.

ABSOLUTE: Or 'Go gentle gales' – *(sings soulfully)* – 'Go, gentle gales....!'

ACRES: Oh no, nothing like it. Odds! Now I remember one of them - *(sings joyously)* "My heart's my own, my will is free".

FAULKLAND: Fool, fool that I am to fix all my happiness on such a trifler! S'death! To make herself the merrymaking musician and singer at a party! What can you say to this sir?

ABSOLUTE: Why, that I should be glad to hear my mistress had been so happy sir.

FAULKLAND: Yes, yes, yes! I am not sorry that she has been happy – yes, I am glad of that. Yet... surely a sympathetic heart would have shown itself at least in the choice of song. However, I do not suppose she has been dancing too?

ACRES: What does the gentleman say about dancing?

ABSOLUTE: He says the lady we speak of dances as well as she sings.

ACRES: Aye truly she does. At our last evening ball –

FAULKLAND: Hell and the devil! There, there! – I told you so! Oh, she thrives in my absence! – dancing! – her whole feelings have been the opposite of mine! I have been anxious, silent, pensive while he has been all song and dance!

ABSOLUTE: For heaven's sake Faulkland. Don't show yourself up. Suppose she has danced, what then? Doesn't society often oblige ...

FAULKLAND: Yes, yes, I'll contain myself - perhaps as you say – it must have been for form's sake. So, Mr Acres, you were praising Miss Melville's manner of dancing the stately minuet hey?

ACRES: Oh yes indeed sir, I can certainly vouch for her delicate manner in the minuet. *(beat)* But what I was going to speak of was her vibrant *country dancing* – odds, loops and twirls! She has such an air with her!

FAULKLAND: What! Defend this Absolute! Country dances! Jogs and reels! Am I to blame now? A minuet I could have forgiven, but *country dances*! Zounds! To be led like a monkey through a string of amorous puppies. If there was one salacious mind in the bunch of them, it will spread like a contagion. Their pulse beats to the lecherous movement of the jig – their sighs impregnate the very air – the atmosphere becomes electrical to love, and each amorous spark darts through each link of the chain! I must leave you. I admit I am somewhat agitated, *(pointing to ACRES)* and this confounded looby has brought it about.

ABSOLUTE: No, but stay Faulkland, and thank Mr Acres for his good news.

FAULKLAND: Damn his news!

(Exit FAULKLAND)

ABSOLUTE: Ha ha ha poor Faulkland. I know Julia loves him beyond measure yet the fop is so full of insecurity he cannot see it. Five minutes ago "nothing on earth could give him a moment's uneasiness"!

ACRES: The gentleman wasn't angry at my praising his mistress, was he?

ABSOLUTE: A little jealous I believe, Bob. That sprightly grace and suggestive manner of yours will cause mischief among the girls here.

ACRES: Ah you joke – ha ha mischief – but you know I am not a free man. My dear Lydia has captivated me. But I must say, she could never abide me when we were in the country because I used to dress so badly. But odds, buttons and brocades I shan't make the same mistake here. I'll make my old clothes know who's master. I shall ditch the hunting frock and leather breeches. Look - my hair has been in training for some time.

ABSOLUTE: Indeed!

ACRES: Aye and although my curly sides are a little restive, my hind-part is looking very dashing.

ABSOLUTE: Oh yes, you'll polish up no doubt.

ACRES: Absolutely. Then I can find my darling Lydia. Odds, dandies and popinjays I'll make her see how polished I am.

ABSOLUTE: Spoken like a man. But pray, Bob, I have observed you have an odd, new kind of swearing.

ACRES: Ha ha! You have noticed it. It's genteel isn't it? There is no meaning in the common oaths and nothing but their antiquity makes them respectable. Instead of by Jove, or by Venus, in order to swear with propriety, the oath should echo the situation. Genteel isn't it?

ABSOLUTE: Very genteel, and very new indeed. I dare say it will supersede all other forms of cursing.

ACRES: Aye, aye. The common 'damns' have had their day! But I expect a message from Mrs Malaprop at my lodgings and I must meet my dear friend Sir Lucious O'Trigger. Adieu Jack, we must meet at night when we shall make many toasts to little Lydia.

ABSOLUTE: That I will with all my heart.

(Exit ACRES, Enter FAG)

FAG: Sir, this is a day for everyone to be out strolling. I found Sir Anthony himself taking the air. He is almost here sir.

(Exit FAG)

ABSOLUTE: Ah my father. Now for a parental lecture, I'm sure.

(Enter SR ANTHONY)

SIR ANTHONY: *(Aside)* There is my lucky son. He will be so full of elation when I tell him I have secured for him the hand of lady Lydia Languish no less!

ABSOLUTE: Sir I am delighted to see you here; and looking so well!

SIR ANTHONY: Well Jack, I am glad to see you. So, you are recruiting here hey?

ABSOLUTE: Yes sir, I am on duty.

SIR ANTHONY: This is fortunate for I was going to write to you on a little matter of business Jack. I have been considering that I may soon grow old and infirm, and shall probably not trouble you for long.

ABSOLUTE: Pardon me sir, I never saw you look more strong and hearty.

SIR ANTHONY: Thank you, my boy. But it is my wish, while I am still living, to see my boy make his mark in the world. I am aware that the income from your commission, and the allowance I provide, are but a small pittance for a lad of your spirit. I have therefore resolved to set you up so that you are nobly independent.

ABSOLUTE: Sir, your kindness overpowers me.

SIR ANTHONY: I am glad you appreciate my sincerity, as indeed you should. I have decided that you shall be master of a large estate in a few weeks.

ABSOLUTE: I cannot express the joyous feelings I have of your generosity. But sir, I presume you would not wish me to quit the army?

SIR ANTHONY: Oh, that shall be as your wife chooses.

ABSOLUTE: My wife, sir?

SIR ANTHONY: Yes, yes, settle that between you. Settle that between you.

ABSOLUTE: A *wife* did you say sir?

SIR ANTHONY: Yes a wife – why, didn't I mention her before?

ABSOLUTE: Not a word of her sir.

SIR ANTHONY: Odso – I must not forget her though. Yes Jack, the independence I was talking about is by marriage – the fortune is saddled with a wife. But I suppose that makes no difference.

ABSOLUTE: Sir you amaze me! How can you suggest such a thing!

SIR ANTHONY: Why! What the devil's the matter with you fool? Just now you were all gratitude and duty.

ABSOLUTE: I was sir – you talked to me of independence and a fortune, but not a word of a wife.

SIR ANTHONY: What difference does that make? Odds life sir! If you have the estate, you must take it as it stands, with the livestock in it.

ABSOLUTE: If my happiness is to be the price, I must decline the purchase. Pray sir, who is the lady?

SIR ANTHONY: What's that to you sir? Come give me your promise to love, and to marry her directly.

ABSOLUTE: Sure, sir this is not very reasonable. To summon my affections for a lady I know nothing of!

SIR ANTHONY: Doubly sure, sir, it is more unreasonable of you to *object* to a lady you know nothing of.

ABSOLUTE: Then sir, I must tell you plainly, that my inclinations are fixed on another – my heart is engaged to an angel.

SIR ANTHONY: Then pray let your heart send an excuse. It is very sorry, but *business* prevents it being with her.

ABSOLUTE: But my vows are pledged to her.

SIR ANTHONY: Then let her discard your vows; they cannot be redeemed.

ABSOLUTE: You must excuse me sir if I tell you once and for all that in this point, I cannot obey you.

SIR ANTHONY: Look here Jack, I have listened to you with patience – I have been cool – quite cool. But take care – you know I am a very flexible man – when I am not thwarted. No-one more easily led – when I have my own way. But don't put me in a frenzy.

29

ABSOLUTE: Sir, I must repeat it – in this I cannot obey you.

SIR ANTHONY: Sir, I won't hear a word. Not a word! Not one word! So give me your promise by a nod. *(Jack does not move)* I'll tell you what Jack – I mean you dog – if you don't by...

ABSOLUTE: You wish me to promise to commit myself to some mass of ugliness!

SIR ANTHONY: Zounds boy! The lady shall be as ugly as I choose. She shall have a hump on each shoulder; her one eye will roll like a marble; she shall have skin like a mummy and the beard of a wizard. I'll make you ogle her all day and sit up all night to write sonnets on her beauty.

ABSOLUTE: This is reason and moderation indeed!

SIR ANTHONY: None of your passion sir! It won't do with me, I promise you.

ABSOLUTE: Indeed sir, I never was cooler in my life.

SIR ANTHONY: That is a confounded lie! I know you are in a passion in your heart; I know you are. You rely upon the meekness of my disposition. Yet take care, I give you six hours and a half to consider this. If you agree, without any condition, to do everything on earth that I choose, why, confound you, I may in time forgive you. If not, zounds! Don't enter the same hemisphere as me! Don't dare breathe the same air or use the same light as me, but get an atmosphere and a sun of your own. I'll strip you of your commission. I'll lodge five shillings in the hands of trustees and you shall live on the interest. I'll disown you. I'll disinherit you. And damn me if I ever call you Jack again!

(Exit SIR ANTHONY)

ABSOLUTE: Gentle, considerate father. What a tender method of giving his opinions on these matters Sir Anthony has! Yet I dare not trust him with the truth. I wonder what old and wealthy hag he wants to bestow on me!

(Enter FAG)

FAG: Sir your father is full of anger. He came down the tearoom stairs eight or ten steps at a time – muttering, growling and thumping the bannisters all the way. I, and the cook's dog were standing bowing at the door. He gave me a rap on the head with his cane, bids me to carry that to my master, then kicking the poor dog, he damned us all as three mangy puppies. Upon my word sir, if I were in your place and found my father such bad company, I should certainly drop his acquaintance.

ABSOLUTE: Cease your impertinence sir. Did you come for nothing more? Stand out of the way!

(ABSOLUTE pushes him out of the way and exits)

FAG: So, Sir Anthony scolds my master; he is too afraid to reply to his father – so he then vents his spleen on poor Fag! When one is vexed by one person, to revenge oneself on another, who happens to come in the way, is the vilest injustice. Ah! It shows the worst temper – the basest…

COOK: *(off stage)*. Mr Fag! Mr Fag! Your master calls you.

FAG: Well, you dirty puppy, you need not bawl so! The meanest disposition! The …

COOK: Quick, quick Mr Fag.

FAG: Quick, quick you impudent jackanapes! Am I to be commanded by you too? *(Exits followed by noises of FAG kicking and beating the COOK)* You little impertinent, insolent, kitchen bred …

Scene 2

(Outside in the park. Enter LUCY)

LUCY: *(speaking in her clever voice)* Poor Acres has finally been dismissed by Mrs Malaprop. Well, I have done one last friendly deed for Mr Acres, letting him know that it was Miss Lydia's love of Beverley that led to his dismissal. *(Looking around)* Sir Lucious is generally more punctual when he expects to hear from his *dear Delia* as he calls her. I do have a slight tinge of conscience from this deceit; but I would not be paid so well if my hero knew that Delia was near fifty, and her own mistress. But still, he is indeed a handsome man. Perhaps it is time I conspired to change his affections in my direction for I will manage his estate far better than he can. I shall stir the pot and see what brews.

(Enter LUCIOUS O'TRIGGER)

SIR LUCIOUS: Hah, Lucy, my little ambassadress - I have been looking for you; I have been on the South parade for half an hour.

LUCY: *(Speaking as a simpleton)* O Gemini! And I have been waiting for your worship here in the park.

SIR LUCIOUS: Faith! Maybe that is the reason we did not meet. How strange that I did not see you go out from Lady Lydia's house with a message, for I was resting at the Parade coffee house opposite and chose the window so that I might not miss you.

LUCY: My stars! Now I'd wager a sixpence I went by while you were taking a nap.

SIR LUCIOUS: Sure enough it must have been that. Well, my little girl, have you got nothing for me?

LUCY: Yes, but I have – I've got a letter for you in my pocket.

SIR LUCIOUS: O faith! I guessed you weren't coming empty handed – well – let me see what the dear creature says.

LUCY: There, Sir Lucious. *(Gives him a letter)*

SIR LUCIOUS: *(Reads) Sir, there is often a sudden fiery impulse in love that creates more demotion in a few seconds than the total sum of elation gathered through many years. Such was the fervour I felt at the first superfluous view of Sir Lucius O'Trigger. Very handsome, upon my word. Female punctuation forbids me to say more; yet let me add that it will give me such hysteria to find that Sir Lucious precipitates my affections - Delia.* Upon my word Lucy your lady is a great mistress of language. Faith, she's quite the queen of the dictionary!

LUCY: Aye sir, a lady of her experience...

SIR LUCIOUS: Experience! What, at seventeen?

LUCY: Oh, true sir – but then she reads so – my stars! How she reads!

SIR LUCIOUS: Faith, she must be a very deep reader to write this way.

LUCY: Ah Sir Lucious. If you were to hear how she talks of you!

SIR LUCIOUS: O tell her I'll make her the best husband in the world, and Lady O'Trigger into the bargain! Although our eyes met just that once across the ballroom floor when she was standing next to that dragon of an aunt, it was love at first sight for us both. I have not been able to talk to her other than through these letters because of the aunt's unwavering protection. We must find a way to get that lady's consent – and do everything properly.

LUCY: Nay Sir Lucious, I thought you weren't rich enough to do things properly!

SIR LUCIOUS: Upon my word young lady, you have hit it. I am so poor that I can't afford to do anything wrong.

LUCY: But sir I must tell you some new news. The aunt has made an arrangement with a gentleman named Captain Absolute. He is to be her husband.

SIR LUCIOUS: How can that be? Her letters are full of love for her Sir Lucious. How can she turn her affections to another so readily?

LUCY: Oh no sir, her affection for you has not changed. She is dead against the match and tells her aunt so to her face. But the aunt and the captain's father are set on it.

SIR LUCIOUS: Zounds! Then by heaven I need to rescue the poor maiden. I need to think this through. Meet me in the evening and I'll give you the answer to this message.

LUCY: But sir, do not let on you knows about the match for it is a secret that I am not supposed to tell. You cannot even let on to your darlin' Delia that you knows.

SIR LUCIOUS: It shall stay between us, upon my honour. I thank you wholeheartedly for your service to me, my pretty girl *(gives her money)*. Here's a little something to buy you a ribbon. Before I leave, take a kiss beforehand to set you off. *(kisses her)*

LUCY: O Lud! Sir Luscious – I never seed such a genman! My lady won't like it if you're so impudent.

SIR LUCIOUS: Faith she will Lucy. That .. pho! what's the word – *modesty* is a quality in a lover more praised by the woman than liked. So if your mistress asks you whether Sir Luscious ever gave you a kiss, tell her fifty my dear!

LUCY: What, would you have me tell a lie?

SIR LUCIOUS: Ah then you baggage. I'll make it the truth right now.

(FAG appears)

LUCY: Oh what a shame now, someone is coming.

SIR LUCIOUS: Oh faith. *(Sees FAG. Exits humming a tune innocently)*

FAG: Well then ma'am. Was I interrupting?

LUCY: O Lud! Now Mr Fag. You flurry one so.

FAG: Come, come Lucy, no one is around, so a little less simplicity and a grain or two more sincerity if you please. Now, I saw you give the baronet a letter from Miss Lydia. Ensign Beverley shall know this – and if he doesn't call him out for a duel – I will.

LUCY: Ha ha ha *(her clever voice)*. You gentlemen's gentlemen are so hasty. That letter was from Mrs Malaprop, simpleton. She is taken with Sir Lucious and I am helping them correspond.

FAG: How! What tastes some people have! But does the young lady have a message for the ensign?

LUCY: No. But, sad news Mr Fag! A worse rival than Acres! Sir Anthony Absolute has proposed his son.

FAG: What! Captain Absolute?

LUCY: Aye sir. I overheard it all.

FAG: Ha ha ha! Upon my word! Very good! I must go back with this news.

LUCY: Well – you may laugh – but it is true, I assure you. *(Going)* But, Mr Fag, tell the young ensign not to be cast down by this.

FAG: Oh, he'll be inconsolable!

LUCY: And tell him not to even think of quarrelling with Captain Absolute.

FAG: Never fear! Never fear!

LUCY: But tell him to keep up his spirits.

FAG: We will! We will!!

(They both leave separately)

Act 3

Scene 1

(The park)

ABSOLUTE: Faith! It is just as Fag told me. My father wants me to marry the very girl I am plotting to run away with! He must not know of my connection with her yet. He will bluster in and disrupt everything. However, I need to take back what I said and assure him of my sincerity. Aha, here he comes, out for his afternoon walk. He looks disagreeably gruff.

(Steps aside. Enters SIR ANTHONY)

SIR ANTHONY: No – I'll die sooner than forgive him. *Die* did I say? No, I'll live another 50 years to plague him. At our last meeting his impudence *almost* made me lose my temper. An obstinate, passionate boy! Who can he take after? This is my fault for putting him at twelve years old into a marching regiment and allowing him fifty pounds a year on top of his pay ever since! But I have done with him – he's nobody's son for me – I will never see him again – never – never.

ABSOLUTE: Now for a penitent face.

SIR ANTHONY: Fellow, get out of my way.

ABSOLUTE: Sir you see a penitent man before you.

SIR ANTHONY: I see an impudent scoundrel before me.

ABSOLUTE: A sincere penitent. I have come, sir, to acknowledge my error and submit entirely to your will.

SIR ANTHONY: What's that?

ABSOLUTE: I have been considering and reflecting on your past goodness and kindness to me.

SIR ANTHONY: Well sir?

ABSOLUTE: I have also been weighing and balancing what you mentioned concerning duty, and obedience, and authority.

SIR ANTHONY: Well puppy?

ABSOLUTE: Well then sir, the result of my reflections is .... A resolution to sacrifice every inclination of my own to your satisfaction.

SIR ANTHONY: Why now, you talk sense – absolute sense – I never heard anything more sensible in my life. Confound you, you shall be Jack again.

ABSOLUTE: I am most happy to be no longer nameless, sir.

SIR ANTHONY: Why then Jack, my dear Jack. I will now inform you who the lady really is. Only your passion and your rage, you silly fellow, prevented me from telling you at first. Prepare yourself Jack, for wonder and rapture – prepare! What do you think of Miss Lydia Languish?

ABSOLUTE: Languish? What the Languishes of Worcestershire?

SIR ANTHONY: Worcestershire! No! Have you never met Mrs Malaprop and her niece, Miss Languish, who moved near to us just before you were last ordered to your regiment?

ABSOLUTE: Malaprop. Languish. I don't remember ever hearing their names before. Now, wait – I think I do recollect something – Languish! Languish! She squints don't she? A little red-haired girl?

SIR ANTHONY: Squints? Red-haired girl! Zounds no.

ABSOLUTE: Then I must have forgot; it can't be the same person.

SIR ANTHONY: Jack, Jack! What do you think of a blooming, romantic seventeen-year-old?

ABSOLUTE: As to that sir, I am quite indifferent. All I desire is to please you.

SIR ANTHONY: Nay, but Jack, such eyes! Such eyes! So innocently wild! So bashfully indecisive. Every glance speaks and kindles some thought of love! Then Jack, her cheeks, her cheeks, Jack! So deeply blushing at the insinuations of her tell-tale eyes. Then Jack, her lips! O

Jack, lips smiling at their own delectability; and if not smiling, even more sweetly delicious when pouting.

ABSOLUTE: *(Aside)* That's her indeed! Well done old gentleman! - And which is to be mine sir, the niece or the aunt?

SIR ANTHONY: Why you unfeeling insensible puppy, I despise you. When I was your age such a description would have made me fly like a rocket! The *aunt* indeed! Odds life! When I ran away with your mother, I would not have touched anything old or ugly to gain an empire.

ABSOLUTE: Not to please your father sir?

SIR ANTHONY: To please my father! Zounds! Not to please.... Oh my father! Odso yes, yes! If my father had indeed desired – that's quite another matter. Though he wasn't the indulgent father that I am Jack.

ABSOLUTE: I am sure sir.

SIR ANTHONY: But Jack, you are not sorry to find your mistress is so beautiful?

ABSOLUTE: Sir, I repeat, if I please you in this affair, that's all I desire. But sir, if you remember, you hinted at a hump or two, one eye, and a few more embellishments of that kind. Now at the risk of feeling ungrateful, I admit I would rather choose a wife of mine to have the usual number of limbs, and a limited quantity of back; and although *one* eye may be very agreeable, since the prejudice has always run in favour of *two*, I would prefer to follow the inclination.

SIR ANTHONY: What a passionless fool you are. No more zeal than a sloth. Odds life! I've a mind to marry the girl myself!

ABSOLUTE: I am entirely at your disposal, sir. If you should think of proposing to Miss Languish yourself, I suppose you would want me to marry the aunt.

SIR ANTHONY: Upon my word Jack! I know your indifference on such a subject must be all a lie. Come along with me and you shall visit the lady immediately. Her eyes shall reel you in. I'll never forgive you if you don't come back stark mad with rapture and impatience. If you don't, egad, I *will* marry the girl myself! *(They leave)*

Scene 2

(Tea rooms. FAULKLAND by himself)

FAULKLAND: Why do I have such a mean, judgemental disposition to my lady Julia; the one person who I love beyond life? What tender, honest joy sparkles in her eyes when we meet! I shall greet her with the same affection. But I must know that she has not been so *very* happy in my absence.

(Enter JULIA)

JULIA: Dearest Faulkland, I am so surprised to see you here.

FAULKLAND: Oh, my darling. I have missed you more than you can imagine. *(Looking at her questioningly, growing cold)* But how are you? Have you been... well?... happy?... Have you missed me as I have missed you?

JULIA: Oh Faulkland, I cannot put into words the yearning I have had in my heart for this moment. Yet do I sense a coldness?

FAULKLAND: I was full of joy on hearing of your health and your arrival here, by your neighbour Acres. But, I was somewhat dampened by him effusively speaking about the high spirits you had enjoyed. About your singing – dancing, and I know not what! For such is my disposition Julia that I should regard every merry moment in your absence as a treason to dedication. The mutual tear that streams down the cheeks of lovers as they part promises that no smile shall live there until they meet again.

JULIA: Can the idle reports of a silly boor weigh in your heart against my steady affection?

FAULKLAND: They have no weight with me Julia; no, no – I am happy if you have been so. Yet just tell me that you did not sing with *mirth*.

JULIA: I can never be happy in your absence. If I appear to be contented, it is to show that my mind holds no doubt of my Faulkland's love. If I was to appear sad, it shows I have set my heart on one person, but that person constantly treats me unfairly and leads me to question my own gullibility. Believe me, Faulkland, I mean not to scold you, when I say that I have often dressed sorrow in smiles in case my friends would guess whose unkindness had caused my tears.

FAULKLAND: You are only ever goodness towards me. Oh, I am a brute when I doubt your true devotion.

JULIA: If ever you find my affections and gratitude diminishing, then may I be scorned and ridiculed.

FAULKLAND: Oh Julia. I wish you had not insisted on mentioning gratitude. Search your feelings Julia; perhaps what you mistake for love is truthfully a warm outpouring of a too thankful heart!

JULIA: Does it matter for what reason I love you – gratitude for saving my life, your mind, physical attraction. What reason must I have?

FAULKAND: If you regard me for my mind then you do not love, but only esteem me. As for my looks, I have often wished I was deformed so I could be convinced that this was not the reason for your attraction.

JULIA: If nature has been kind to bestow fine features on a man, he should laugh them off as unimportant. Yes I have seen vain men who perhaps in looks may rank above you, but my heart has never let my eyes consider them.

FAULKLAND: That is an atrocious thing for you to say Julia. If you loved me as I wished you did, even if I was a one-eyed hunchback, you would think no other man outranked me in looks.

JULIA: I see you are determined to be unkind. The contract of marriage that my poor father bound us in gives you more than a lover's privilege.

FAULKLAND: Again Julia you raise ideas that feed my doubt. Perhaps your high regard for your father's solemn contract has restrained you from making a worthier choice of lover. How can I be sure that if you were not *bound* to me, that I should still have been the object of your persevering love.

JULIA: Then try me now. Let us say we are as free as strangers with no obligation. Now that I am free, I assure you my heart feels no more liberty. My love for you remains unchanged!

FAULKLAND: There now! So hasty and anxious to be unbound Julia. If your love for me were fixed and ardent, you would not allow yourself to be free, even if I wished it.

JULIA: Oh, you torture me to the heart. I cannot bear it!

FAULKLAND: I do not mean to distress you my darling. But women are not used to weighing and separating the motives of their affections. Gratitude or family duty may sometimes be mistaken for pleadings of the heart. I do not wish to boast, but let me say that one would find it difficult to dislike my appearance, age, character and indeed my fortune. When these appealing ingredients combine with a large spoonful of duty, caution would have to question the reasons for the birth of love.

JULIA: I don't know where your insinuations are leading, but as they seem to contrive to insult me, I will spare you the regret you will feel later. Sir, I have given you no cause for this!

(JULIA goes through a door to a side-room in tears)

FAULKLAND: In tears! Julia, stay, stay just for a moment. The door is locked! I hear her sobbing! What a brute I am to hurt her like this. But wait – yes – she is coming now; how little resolution there is in a woman! How a few soft words can turn them! No, faith! She is *not* coming. Why Julia – my love – say that you forgive me. Now this is being *too* resentful. Wait – she *is* coming – I thought she would – no *steadiness* in anything! Her going away must have been a mere trick then – I won't let her see I was hurt by it – I'll pretend to be indifferent *(hums a tune and listens)*. No, zounds! She's *not* coming! I deserve it. It was barbarous to quarrel with her tenderness! I'll wait until her resentment subsides. And if I distress her so again, may I lose her forever, and be linked to some ancient fishwife, whose gnawing passions and mean temper, shall make me curse my foolishness, half the day and all the night.

(FAULKLAND leaves)

41

Scene 3

(Tea rooms. MRS MALAPROP and CAPTAIN ABSOLUTE)

MRS MALAPROP: You being Sir Anthony's son, Captain, would itself be a sufficient accommodation but from the negligence of your appearance I can see you are a fine character.

ABSOLUTE: Permit me to say madam that I have never had the pleasure of seeing Miss Languish. My principal motive in this affair is the honour of being allied to Mrs Malaprop, whose intellectual accomplishments and elegant manners are highly regarded.

MRS MALAPROP: Sir, you do me infinite honour! Please sit-down Captain. Ah, few gentlemen these days know how to value the ineffectual qualities in a woman! Few think how a little knowledge becomes a gentlewoman. Men only revere the worthless flower of beauty!

ABSOLUTE: That is true indeed ma'am. Yet I fear ladies must share the blame. They think our admiration of beauty so great, that having knowledge would be superfluous. Thus, like garden trees they seldom show fruit until time has robbed them of the more misleading blossom. Few like Mrs Malaprop, and the orange tree, are rich in both at once!

MRS MALAPROP: Sir, you overpower me with good breeding. You are the very pineapple of politeness. You are aware, Captain, that this giddy girl has somehow contrived to fix her affections on a beggarly ensign, whom none of us have seen.

ABSOLUTE: Oh yes, I have heard of the silly affair. I'm not at all prejudiced against her on *that* account.

MRS MALAPROP: You are very good, Captain. I am sure I have done everything in my power since I exploded the affair. Long ago I inducted her never to think of that fellow again. I have since laid Sir Anthony's

42

preposition before her – but I am sorry to say she seems resolved to refuse every abduction that I give her.

ABSOLUTE: It must be very distressing indeed ma'am.

MRS MALAPROP: Oh it gives me the hydrostatics to such a degree! I thought she had persisted from corresponding with him; but behold this very day, I have infected another letter from the fellow! I believe I have it in my pocket.

ABSOLUTE: *(aside)* Oh the devil! My last note.

MRS MALAPROP: Aye here it is.

ABSOLUTE: *(aside)* Aye my note indeed! Oh, that little traitress Lucy.

MRS MALAPROP: There, perhaps you know the writing?

ABSOLUTE: I think I have seen this hand before – yes, I certainly must have seen this hand before.

MRS MALAPROP: Read it Captain.

ABSOLUTE: *(reads) My soul's idol. My adored Lydia!* Very tender indeed!

MRS MALAPROP: Tender! Aye and profane too, upon my conscience!

ABSOLUTE: *I am excessively alarmed at the intelligence you sent me. The more so as my new rival –*

MRS MALAPROP: That's you sir.

ABSOLUTE: *- has universally the character of being an accomplished gentleman, and a man of honour.* Well, that's handsome enough.

MRS MALAPROP: Oh, the fellow has some skill in writing.

ABSOLUTE: That he has.

MRS MALAPROP: But go on sir, you'll see presently.

ABSOLUTE: *As for the old weather-beaten she-dragon who guards you.* What can he mean by that?

MRS MALAPROP: Me, sir, *me* - he means *me* there – what do you think now? But go on a little further.

43

ABSOLUTE: Impudent scoundrel! *It shall be hard, but I shall evade her vigilance, as I am told the same ridiculous vanity, which makes her dress up her coarse features, and deck her dull chat with hard words which she does not understand –*

MRS MALAPROP: There, sir! An attack on my language! What do you think of that! An aversion upon my parts of speech! Was ever there such a brute! Certainly, as I reprehend anything in this world, when it comes to words, I am exceedingly fallacious, and can be relied on to produce a nice derangement of epitaphs!

ABSOLUTE: He deserves to be hanged and quartered! Let me see – *same ridiculous vanity –*

MRS MALAPROP: You need not read it again sir.

ABSOLUTE: I beg pardon ma'am – *does also lay her open to the grossest deceptions from flattery.* An impudent coxcomb! *So, I have a scheme to see you shortly with the old hag's consent, and even to make her a go-between in our interview.* – Was ever there such confidence!

MRS MALAPROP: Did you ever hear anything like it? He'll evade my vigilance, will he? Ha ha! He's very likely to enter these doors! We'll see who can plot the best!

ABSOLUTE: So we will ma'am – so we will. A conceited puppy, ha ha ha. Perhaps I could see the lady for a few minutes? I should like to experience her temper a little. Is she at your lodgings?

MRS MALAPROP: No sir, she is in the upstairs room. I am sure she is prepared for a visit of this kind, but there is a decorum in these matters.

ABSOLUTE: O Lord! She won't mind *me* – tell her that Beverley …

MRS MALAPROP: Sir?

ABSOLUTE: (*Aside*) Gently, good tongue.

MRS MALAPROP: What did you say about Beverley?

ABSOLUTE: Oh, I was going to propose that you should tell her, by way of jest, that it is Beverley who was below – she'd come down fast enough then – ha ha ha!

44

MRS MALAPROP: It would be a trick she well deserves – besides you know the fellow tells her he'll get my consent to see her – ha ha ha! Let him if he can. He'll make me *go-between in their interviews!* – ha ha ha! His impudence is truly ridiculous.

ABSOLUTE: It is very ridiculous upon my soul ma'am, ha ha ha!

MRS MALAPROP: I'll go and get the little hussy. She'll know that Captain Absolute has come to visit her. And I'll make her behave as becomes a young woman.

ABSOLUTE: As you please, ma'am.

MRS MALAPROP: For the present, captain, your servant. *Evade my vigilance!* Ha ha ha! *(Exit)*

ABSOLUTE: Ha ha ha! Perhaps I might throw off all disguise at once and seize my prize beauty. But such is Lydia's fickleness that if I was to free her from my deception then I would probably lose her. *(Walks aside, and seems engaged looking outside)*

(Enter LYDIA)

LYDIA: Surely nothing can be more dreadful than to be obliged to listen to the loathsome addresses of a stranger to one's heart. There stands the hated rival – an officer too. But oh, how unlike my Beverley! I wonder why he does not speak. Truly he seems a very negligent wooer! I'll speak first… Mr Absolute.

ABSOLUTE: Madam. *(Turns round)*

LYDIA: O heavens, Beverley!

ABSOLUTE: Hush! Hush, my life! Softly! Do not be surprised!

LYDIA: I am astonished! And so terrified! For heaven's sake, how are you here?

ABSOLUTE: Briefly – I have deceived your aunt. I was informed that my new rival was to visit here this afternoon. So I kept him away and have passed myself off for Captain Absolute.

LYDIA: Oh charming! And she really takes you for young Absolute?

ABSOLUTE: Oh she's convinced of it.

LYDIA: Ha ha ha! I can't help laughing to think how her keen judgement has been so outwitted.

ABSOLUTE: But we waste our precious moments. Such another opportunity may not occur. So let me implore my benevolent angel to fix the time when I may rescue her from undeserved maltreatment.

LYDIA: Will you then, Beverley, consent to forfeit that portion of my wealth that flies away on the wings of love.

ABSOLUTE: Oh come to me – rich only in loveliness. Bring nothing to me but your affection. That will be generous of you, Lydia, for as you know, it is the only dower your poor Beverley can repay.

LYDIA: *(Aside)* How persuasive are his words! How charming will poverty be with him!

ABSOLUTE: Ah my soul, what a life will we live! Love shall be our support! The gloom of adversity shall make the flame of our pure love glow bright. By heavens! I fling all fortune aside and say the world gives me no happiness except for here *(embracing her)*. *(Aside)* If she can resist me now then the Devil is on her side.

LYDIA: *(Almost convinced but unsure)* Now I could fly with him to the Antipodes, but my persecution has not yet pushed me over the edge.

MRS MALAPROP: *(Appears at the door. Aside)* I'm impatient to know how the little hussy behaves herself.

ABSOLUTE: So pensive, Lydia! Has your warmth dwindled?

MRS MALAPROP: *(Aside)* Warmth dwindled! So, she has been in a passionate rage I suppose.

LYDIA: No – nor could it ever while I have life.

MRS MALAPROP: *(Aside)* Ill-tempered she-devil. She'll be in a passionate rage all her life will she?

LYDIA: Don't think that the idle threats of my ridiculous aunt can ever have any weight with me.

MRS MALAPROP: *(Aside)* Very dutiful, upon my word!

LYDIA: Let her choice be Captain Absolute, but Beverley is mine.

MRS MALAPROP: *(Aside)* I am astonished at her declaration! To his face! This to his face!

ABSOLUTE: *(Kneeling)* Therefore let me reiterate my desire for you

MRS MALAPROP: *(Aside)* Aye, poor young man! Down on his knees entreating for pity. I can contain myself no longer. *(Reveals herself)* Why you vixen! I overheard you!

ABSOLUTE: *(Aside)* Oh confound her vigilance!

MRS MALAPROP: Captain Absolute – I don't know how to apologise for her shocking rudeness.

ABSOLUTE: *(Aside)* So, all is safe it seems. *(Aloud)* I have hopes, madam that time will bring the young lady…

MRS MALAPROP: Oh, there's nothing to be hoped for from her! She's as headstrong as an allegory on the banks of the Nile.

LYDIA: Now madam, what do you accuse me of now?

MRS MALAPROP: Why you unblushing rebel – didn't you tell this gentleman to his face that you loved another better? Didn't you say you would never be his?

LYDIA: No, madam – I did not.

MRS MALAPROP: Good heavens, Lydia! You ought to know that lying doesn't become a young woman! Didn't you boast that the layabout Beverley possessed your heart? Tell me the truth I say!

LYDIA: That is true ma'am, and no one but Beverley.

MRS MALAPROP: Stop, stop! You shall not be so rude.

ABSOLUTE: No, please Mrs Malaprop, don't stop the young lady's speech. She's very welcome to say these things – it does not hurt *me* in the least, I assure you.

MRS MALAPROP: You are too good Captain, *too* amiably patient. But you come with me Miss. We will meet again soon Captain. Remember what we have arranged,

ABSOLUTE: I shall ma'am.

MRS MALAPROP: Come, take your leave gracefully of the gentleman.

LYDIA: May every blessing go to my Beverley – my beloved *Bev* ...

MRS MALAPROP: Hussy! I'll choke the word in your throat! Come along – come along.

(They leave separately. ABSOLUTE kissing his hand to LYDIA, MRS MALAPROP stopping her from speaking)

Scene 4

(In the park. ACRES and DAVID)

ACRES: What a fine day. David. You must thank your master for allowing you to assist me.

DAVID: Not at all sir. I believe my master feels I am a little too much of a jack-a-dandy. He seemed only too pleased to release me.

ACRES: Indeed, well his loss is my gain, David. Do you think my outfit suits me?

DAVID: You are quite another creature, believe me sir, upon my word!

ACRES: Dress *does* make a difference David.

DAVID: It is an enormous difference. Why if you were to go back home now, I am certain the old lady would not recognise you; Master Butler would not believe his own eyes, and Mrs Pickle would cry 'Lord preserve me'. I would bet a fortune that there ain't a dog in the house who would not bark!

ACRES: Aye, David, there's nothing like polishing.

DAVID: So I says of your honour's boots but the boy never listens to me.

ACRES: But David, did you speak to Mr De-La-Grace? I must boost my French dance technique.

DAVID: I'll call again sir.

ACRES. Do – and see if there are any letters for me at the post office.

DAVID. I will. Zounds sir, I can't help looking at your head! You appear so different. If I hadn't of been there at the cooking, I would never have known the dish myself. But I must be off, sir.

(Exit DAVID. ACRES comes forward practising a dance step)

ACRES: Sink, slide, point... confound the inventors of French country dances – they are as bad as algebra to us gentlemen. I can walk a minuet easily when I am forced to, and I am well regarded in *simple* country dances. But odds, jigs and promenades, when men and women are crossing over, hopping and running round in circles, it is quite beyond me! I have trueborn English legs and my feet have the most anti-gallic toes.

(Enter SIR LUCIOUS O'TRIGGER)

SIR LUCIOUS: Mr Acres, there you are. I am delighted to embrace you. My my, you look particularly fine this afternoon!

ACRES: Why thank you my dear Sir Lucious.

SIR LUCIOUS: Now my friend, what has brought you to Bath so suddenly?

ACRES: Faith, I have followed Cupid's bow and find myself in a quagmire! In short, I have been very ill-used, Sir Lucious. I don't choose to mention names, but consider me a very ill-used gentleman.

SIR LUCIOUS: Pray, what is the cause. I ask for no names.

ACRES: Listen to this Sir Lucious. I have fallen deeply as possible in love with a young lady. Her family approve of me – I follow her to Bath – send word of my arrival – and then receive an answer that the lady has disposed of me. This, Sir Lucious, is what I call being ill-treated.

SIR LUCIOUS: Very poorly treated, upon my conscience. Pray can you tell me the cause of this disposal.

ACRES: Why yes. Here is the cause. She has another lover. One *Beverley*, who I am told is now in Bath. Odds, slanders and lies, he must be at the bottom of it.

SIR LUCIOUS: So, there is a rival for the lady. And you think he has displaced you unfairly?

ACRES: Unfairly! To be sure he has. He could never have done it fairly.

SIR LUCIOUS: Then for sure you know what is to be done!

ACRES: Upon my soul, I have no idea.

SIR LUCIOUS: We wear no swords in Bath; but you do understand me.

ACRES: What! Fight him!

SIR LUCIOUS: Aye to be sure. What else can I mean?

ACRES: But he has given me no provocation!

SIR LUCIOUS: I think he has given you the greatest provocation in the world. Can a man commit a more heinous offence against another than to fall in love with the same woman? Oh, by my soul, it is the most unpardonable breach of friendship!

ACRES: Breach of friendship! Yes, yes, but I have no acquaintance with this man, I have never seen him in my life!

SIR LUCIOUS: That's no argument at all – that means he has less right to take such a liberty.

ACRES: Gad, that's true. I grow full of anger, Sir Lucious. I am exceedingly fired up. Odds, hilts and blades! I find a man can have a great deal of valour in him, and not know it. *(Apprehensive)* But I am not sure in this case if I have right on my side.

SIR LUCIOUS: What the devil does *right* have to do with it when *honour* is concerned. Do you think Achilles, or Alexander the Great ever enquired whether a thing was *right*? No, upon my soul, they drew their broadswords and left the attorneys to settle the justice of it.

ACRES: Your words stir my heart like a grenadier's march. I believe courage must be catching! I certainly do feel a kind of valour rising. Odds, flints, flash-pans and triggers. I'll challenge him at once.

SIR LUCIOUS: Ah my little friend! If we were in my own Blunderbuss Hall, I could show you a prodigious range of my ancestors, every one of whom killed his man! For though my estate slowly slips through my fingers, I thank heaven for our honour, and the family portraits are as fresh as ever.

ACRES: Oh Sir Lucious! I have military ancestors too! Odds, balls and barrels, say no more – I am braced for it. The thunder of your words has soured the milk of human kindness in my breast!

SIR LUCIOUS: Come, come, there must be no passion at all in the case – these things should always be done civilly.

ACRES: I must be in a passion Sir Lucious – I must be in a rage. Dear Sir Lucious, let me be in a rage. Come here's a pencil and paper. *(Sits down to write)*. We will draft a challenge. How shall I begin? Odds bullets and blades.

SIR LUCIOUS: Please compose yourself.

ACRES: Come – shall I begin with an oath? Do, Sir Lucious let me begin with a damme!

SIR LUCIOUS: Pho! Pho! Do the thing decently and like a Christian. Begin now – *Sir* –

ACRES: That's too civil by half

SIR LUCIOUS: *To prevent confusion that may arise* –

ACRES: Good –

SIR LUCIOUS: *From our both addressing the same lady* –

ACRES: Aye – there's the reason – *(Writing) same lady.* Good.

SIR LUCIOUS: *I shall expect the honour of your company* –

ACRES: Zounds! I'm not asking him to dinner.

SIR LUCIOUS: Pray be easy.

ACRES: Well then, *honour of your company.*

SIR LUCIOUS: *To settle our claim* –

ACRES: Good.

SIR LUCIOUS: Let me see, yes, Kingsmead Fields will do – *in Kingsmead Fields.*

51

ACRES: So that's done. I'll write it up later in a good bold hand! I wish the ink was red! My own crest – a hand and a dagger – will be the seal.

SIR LUCIOUS: You see how this little explanation will put a stop at once to all confusion or misunderstanding that may arise between you.

ACRES: Aye, we fight to prevent a misunderstanding.

SIR LUCIOUS: Now, I'll leave you to fix your own time. Make it this evening. Then let the worst be done and it will be off your mind tomorrow.

ACRES: Very true.

SIR LUCIOUS: Now I also have news to tell you in confidence. I shall be undertaking a similar affair. Like you Mr Acres, I am in love with the most beautiful creature in the country. No names. We correspond secretly, for her situation is such that we cannot presently meet in person. Now I find that there is a carefree captain here who aims to place himself between me and the passions of this lady. That situation will shortly be resolved through an honourable discussion with the point of my blade.

ACRES: Odds, shock and coincidence! By my valour, I should like to see you fight first! Odds, life! I should like to see you kill him, if only to get a little lesson.

SIR LUCIOUS: I shall be very proud of instructing you. Well, I must go, but remember now, when you meet your antagonist, let your courage be keen, but at the same time as polished as your sword.

(The leave separately)

Act 4

Scene 1

(In the park. LUCY walks on. Characters come and go swiftly as they address the audience, ignoring each other)

LUCY: Ladies and gentlemen. Nay, I shall call you Friends since we have journeyed together so tumultuously. *[To audience]* Sir, madam, are we not friends now?

Welcome back then friends. Have you quaffed a flagon of ale and feel ready to resolve our conundrum of whiffle whaffle? Let us first help to unravel any confusion or memory loss caused by yon flagon. First my lady Lydia...

(Exit Lucy, Enter Lydia)

LYDIA: My darling Ensign Beverley has tricked my aunt, Mrs Malaprop, that he is Captain Absolute, allowing us to meet. Oh, I am completely smitten and feel I shall elope with him soon...

(Exit Lydia, Enter ABSOLUTE)

ABSOLUTE: I am being dragged by my father Sir Anthony to see Mrs Malaprop and my Lydia. Lydia believes I am Beverley yet will be forced to meet me as myself. I am at a loss what to do.

(Exit ABSOLUTE, Enter FAULKLAND)

FAULKLAND: I fear my lack of trust has lost the one person in life I am destined to marry. How can I be such a fool to the kindest, gentlest most beautiful person in the world. Are singing and dancing so terrible. Nay... *(getting annoyed)* yet country dancing!

(Exit FAULKLAND, Enter ACRES and SIR LUSCIOUS)

ACRES: I am set to challenge this dog Beverley, who has unfairly stolen my darling Lydia. My good friend Sir Luscious, you have so riled me that I feel invincible. Yet... I have never fought a person in my life. Perhaps I should reconsider....

SIR LUSCIOUS: Nay sir! The contest must be done. You shall learn from my fight with this rascally Captain and we shall both prevail! And I can at last meet in person the lady whose beauty and wordsmithing so enraptures me.

(Exit SIR LUSCIOUS)

(Tea Rooms. DAVID and ACRES)

DAVID: Heavens forbid, sir! I would never do such a thing. No Sir Lucious O'Trigger would ever make me fight when I am not of that mind. Oons, what will your mother say when she hears.

ACRES: Ah David! If you had heard Sir Lucious! Odds, sparks and flames, he would have raised your valour.

DAVID: Indeed, he would not. I hate such bloodthirsty devils. Look master, if you'd wanted a bout at boxing or fighting with a quarterstaff, I would never ask you to cry off. But with your cursed swords and pistols, I never knew any good come of them.

ACRES: But consider my honour, David, my honour! I must be very careful of my honour!

DAVID: Aye by heavens, I would indeed be very careful of it. And I think in return my *honour* couldn't do less than to be very careful of *me*.

ACRES: Odds, blades David! No gentleman will ever risk the loss of his honour!

DAVID: I say then, *honour* would be civil never to risk the loss of the *gentleman*. Look master, this honour seems to be a marvellous false friend. Sir, imagine I was a gentleman (which thank God no one can say of me), and my honour makes me kill another gentleman. Who profits from it? Why, my *honour* does. But what if he kills me? Zounds! I go to the worms, and my honour whips over to my enemy.

ACRES: No David – in that case – odds, crowns and laurels! Your honour follows you to the grave.

DAVID: Now, that's just the place where I could do without it.

ACRES: Zounds David. You're a coward! It doesn't suit my valour to listen to you. What, shall I disgrace my ancestors? Think of that, David. Think what it would be to disgrace my ancestors!

DAVID: Pardon me sir but the surest way of not disgracing them is to keep as long as you can out of their company. Look now Master, you should not join them in such haste with an ounce of lead in your brains. Our ancestors are very good people, but they are the last people I should choose to visit.

ACRES: But David, you don't think there is such a very, *very*, great danger, hey? Odds, life! People often fight without any mischief done!

DAVID: By heavens, I think it is ten to one against you! Oons! You are about to meet some lion-headed fellow, with his damned double-barrelled swords, and cut and thrust pistols! Those are such desperate bloody-minded weapons! Since I was a child, I could never abide them. There is never such a merciless beast in the world as your loaded pistol.

ACRES: Zounds I *won't* be afraid. Odds, fire and fury you shan't make me afraid! Here is the challenge, and I have sent for my dear friend Jack Absolute to carry the message for me.

DAVID: Aye, in the name of mischief let him be the messenger. For I wouldn't take it for the best horse in your stable. By heavens, it doesn't even look like a normal letter. It is a malicious looking letter, and I warrant smells of gunpowder like a soldier's pouch. Oon's it looks like it is about to go off.

ACRES: Out you numbskull! You have the valour of a grasshopper.

DAVID: Well, I say no more. It will be sad news back at your manor. How your maid Phyllis will howl when she hears of it. She has no idea what shooting is about to take place.

ACRES: It won't do David – I am determined to fight. Get along out of my sight you cowardly, croaking raven

DAVID: *(Whimpering)*. Goodbye, Master.

(Exit DAVID, Enter ABSOLUTE)

ABSOLUTE: What's the matter Bob?

ACRES: A vile, sheep-hearted blockhead! If I hadn't the valour of St George and the dragon to boot –

ABSOLUTE: I believe you wanted to see me, Bob.

ACRES: Oh – there! *(Gives him the challenge letter)*

ABSOLUTE: *(Aside) To Ensign Beverley.* So, what's going on now? - Well, what's this?

ACRES: A challenge!

ABSOLUTE: Indeed! Why, you won't fight him will you Bob?

ACRES: Egad but I will Jack. Sir Lucious has stirred me up. He has left me full of rage, and I'll fight this evening, so my passion won't diminish.

ABSOLUTE: But what do I have to do with this?

ACRES: Well, I think you know something of this fellow. So, I want you to find him for me and give him this challenge.

ABSOLUTE: Well, give it to me and trust me he will get it.

ACRES: Thank you my dear friend. My dear Jack. This is not too much trouble?

ABSOLUTE: Not in the least. No trouble in the world I assure you.

ACRES: You are very kind. What it is to have a friend! You couldn't be my second could you jack?

ABSOLUTE: Why no Bob, not in this affair. It would not be quite so proper.

ACRES: Well then, I must get my friend Sir Lucious. I shall have your good wishes however Jack.

ABSOLUTE: Until he meets you, believe me. Now I must go – I must meet Sir Anthony Absolute. Well, my little hero, I wish you every success.

ACRES: A moment Jack. If Beverley asks you what kind of man your friend Acres is, tell him I am a devil of a fellow, will you Jack?

ABSOLUTE: To be sure I shall. I'll say you are a determined dog, hey Bob!

ACRES: Aye, do, do. And if that frightens him, egad perhaps he may not come. So, tell him I generally kill a man a week will you, Jack?

ABSOLUTE: I will, I will. I'll say you are called in the country 'Fighting Bob'!

ACRES: Right, right. It's all to prevent mischief, for I don't want to take his life just to clear my honour.

ABSOLUTE: No? That's very kind of you.

ACRES: Why, you don't wish me to kill him, do you Jack?

ABSOLUTE: No, upon my soul, I do not. Adieu *(Going)*

ACRES: Wait, wait Jack. You may add that you never saw me in such a rage before – a most devouring rage!

ABSOLUTE: I will, I will.

ACRES: Remember Jack – a determined dog!

ABSOLUTE: Aye, aye, 'Fighting Bob'.

(They both leave separately)

Scene 2

(Tea rooms. MRS MALAPROP and LYDIA)

MRS MALAPROP: Why, tell me why you object to him? Isn't he a handsome man? A genteel man?

LYDIA: *(aside)* She does not know who she is praising! So is Beverley, ma'am.

MRS MALAPROP: No caparisons miss if you please! Caparisons don't become a young woman. No, Captain Absolute is indeed a fine gentleman!

LYDIA: *(Aside)* Aye the Captain Absolute *you* have seen.

MRS MALAPROP: And he is *so* well bred - *so* full of cheerfulness and admiration! So well-spoken too. His presence is so noble and aromatic.

LYDIA: *(Aside)* How enraged will she be when she discovers her mistake!

MRS MALAPROP: *(Looking outside)* I see Sir Anthony and Captain Absolute are here. Now Lydia, I insist on your good breeding at least, though you have forgotten your duty.

LYDIA: Madam, I have told you my resolution. I shall not only give him no encouragement, but I won't even look at him. *(Flings herself into a chair with her face from the door.)*

(Enter SIR ANTHONY and ABSOLUTE)

SIR ANTHONY: Here we are Mrs Malaprop. Here to mitigate the frowns of unrelenting beauty. Zounds, the difficulty I had to bring this fellow. I don't know what's the matter but if I had not held him by force he would have given me the slip.

MRS MALAPROP: You have had so much trouble Sir Anthony in this affair. I am ashamed of the cause! *(Aside to LYDIA)* Lydia, Lydia rise I implore you. Pay your respects!

SIR ANTHONY: I hope, madam, that Miss Languish has reflected on the worth of this gentleman, the respect due to her aunt's choice, and *my* wishes. *(Aside to ABSOLUTE)* Now, Jack, speak to her!

ABSOLUTE: *(Aside)* What the devil shall I do? – You see sir, she won't even look at me whilst you are here. I knew she wouldn't! Let me beseech you, sir, to leave us together.

(ABSOLUTE seems to remonstrate with his father)

LYDIA: *(Aside)* I wonder that I haven't heard my aunt exclaim yet! Surely she can't yet have looked at him! Perhaps their regimental uniforms are alike and she is a little blind.

SIR ANTHONY: I say sir, I won't be made to leave here yet.

MRS MALAPROP: I am sorry to say, sir, that my effluence over my niece is very small. *(Aside to LYDIA)* Turn around Lydia, I am embarrassed for you!

SIT ANTHONY: Will Miss Languish speak of why she takes a dislike to my son? *(Aside to ABSOLUTE)* Why don't you begin Jack. Speak, puppy speak!

MRS MALAPROP: It is impossible, Sir Anthony, that she can have any reason. *(Aside to LYDIA)* Answer hussy! Why don't you answer?

SIR ANTHONY: Then madam, I trust that a childish predisposition will be no bar to Jack's happiness. *(Aside to ABSOLUTE)* Zounds boy! Why don't you speak?

LYDIA: *(Aside)* I think my lover seems as little inclined to conversation as myself. How strangely blind my aunt must be!

59

ABSOLUTE: Ahem! Ahem! – madam – Ahem! *(ABSOLUTE attempts to speak, then returns to SIR ANTHONY)* Faith, sir, I am so perplexed! And so, so, confused! I told you I would be so sir. I knew it – the – the torrent of my passion entirely takes away my presence of mind.

SIR ANTHONY: But it doesn't take away your voice, fool, does it? Go up and speak to her directly. Unlock your jaws, boy, or –

(ABSOLUTE draws near LYDIA)

ABSOLUTE: *(Aside)* By heavens, I hope she is too sullen to look round! I must disguise my voice. *(Speaks to her in a low hoarse tone)* Will Miss Languish listen to the mild pleas of true love. Will you –

SIR ANTHONY: What the devil ails the fellow? Why don't you speak out? Not stand croaking like a frog with a sore throat!

ABSOLUTE: The – the – excess of my awe, and my – my – modesty, quite choke me!

SIR ANTHONY: I'll tell you what Jack; if you don't speak out directly, and smoothly too, I shall be in such a rage! Mrs Malaprop, I wish the lady would favour us with something more than a side front!

(Mrs MALAPROP Seems to chide LYDIA)

ABSOLUTE: *(Aside)* So – all will be out I see! *(Goes up to LYDIA, speaks softly)* Be not surprised, my Lydia. Suppress all surprise for the moment.

LYDIA: *(Aside)* Heavens! It is Beverley's voice! Surely he can't have fooled Sir Anthony too! *(Looks round by degrees, then starts up)* Is this possible! My Beverley! How can this be? My Beverley!

ABSOLUTE: *(Aside)* Ah, it is all over!

SIR ANTHONY: Beverley! The devil – Beverley! What can the girl mean? This is my son, Jack Absolute!

MRS MALAPROP: For shame, hussy, for shame! Your head is so full of that fellow that you always have him in your eyes. Beg Captain Absolute's pardon immediately.

LYDIA: I see no Captain Absolute, but my beloved Beverley!

SIR ANTHONY: Zounds! The girl's mad – her brain's turned by reading!

MRS MALAPROP: On my conscience! I believe so! What do you mean by Beverley, hussy! You saw Captain Absolute earlier today. There he is – your husband that shall be.

LYDIA: With all my soul ma'am – how can I refuse my Beverley –

SIR ANTHONY: Oh she's as mad as Bedlam! Or has this fellow been playing a rogue's trick! Come here boy! Who the devil are you?

ABSOLUTE: Faith, sir. I am not quite clear myself, but I'll endeavour to recollect.

SIR ANTHONY: Are you my son or not? Answer for your mother, you dog, if you won't for me.

MRS MALAPROP: Why, sir, who are you? Oh mercy! I begin to suspect...

ABSOLUTE: *(Aside)* Will the power of impudence befriend me! – Sir Anthony, most certainly I am your wife's son; and that I sincerely believe myself to be *yours* also. Mrs Malaprop, I am your most respectful admirer – and shall be proud to be an affectionate nephew. I need not tell my Lydia that she sees her faithful *Beverley*, who, knowing the singular generosity of her temper, assumed the name, and a station below himself. During that time he has proved a test of a love that is not influenced by considerations of personal advantage. And now he now hopes to enjoy that love in a more elevated character.

LYDIA: *(Sullenly)* So! There will be no elopement after all!

SIR ANTHONY: Upon my soul Jack! You are a very impudent fellow! To do you justice, I think I never saw more accomplished confidence in such a situation!

ABSOLUTE: Oh you flatter me sir. I am just trying to keep my dignity.

SIR ANTHONY: Well I am glad you are not the dull insensible rascal you pretended to be! So this was your *penitence*, your *duty* and *obedience*! I thought it was damned sudden! You *never heard their names before*, not you! *If you could please me in the affair, it was all you desired! (Pointing to Lydia) She squints, doesn't she – a little red-haired girl –* hey! Why you scamp – I wonder you aren't ashamed to hold up your head!

ABSOLUTE: It is with much difficulty sir. I am confused – very much confused as you must perceive.

MRS MALAPROP: O Lord Sir Anthony. The light dawns on me! Hey! How! What! Captain, did *you* write the letters then? What! Am I to thank *you* for the elegant description of 'an old weather-beaten she-dragon' hey? O mercy! Was it *you* that reflected on my parts of speech?

ABSOLUTE: *(Aside to SIR ANTHONY)* Dear sir, my dignity will be overpowered if you don't assist me.

SIR ANTHONY: Come, come Mrs Malaprop. We must forget and forgive. Odds, life, matters have taken such a turn for the better all of a sudden, that I find myself so good-humoured and forgiving, hey, Mrs Malaprop!

MRS MALAPROP: Well, Sir Anthony, since *you* desire it, we will not anticipate the past. So then young people, retrospection will now be all in the future.

SIR ANTHONY: Come, we must leave them together Mrs Malaprop; they long to fly into each other's arms, I warrant. Jack, aren't her cheeks as I said, hey! And her eyes, you rogue, and her lips hey? Come. Mrs Malaprop, we'll not disturb their tenderness. *(Sings)* 'Youth's the season made for joy'. Odds. Life I'm in such good spirits, I could do anything! *(Gives his hand to MRS MALAPROP)* Permit me, ma'am – *(Sings)* Tol-de-rol – gad I should like a little fooling myself - tol-de-rol-de-rol!

(Exit singing and handling MRS MALAPROP. LYDIA sits sullenly in her chair)

ABSOLUTE: *(Aside)* So much thought does not bode well for me. – So grave Lydia!

LYDIA: Sir!

ABSOLUTE: *(Aside)* So! – egad! I thought as much! That damned monosyllable has frozen me! - What Lydia, now that we are happy with our family's consent –

LYDIA: *Family's consent,* indeed!

ABSOLUTE: Come, come, we must put aside some of our romance – a little wealth and comfort may be endured after all. And as for your fortune, the lawyers shall make such settlements as –

LYDIA: *Lawyers!* I hate lawyers!

ABSOLUTE: Nay, then. We will not wait for their bureaucracy, but instantly procure the marriage licence, and –

LYDIA: *Licence!* I hate licence!

ABSOLUTE: O my love, don't be so unkind! Let me entreat you – *(Kneeling)*

LYDIA: Pshaw! – What does kneeling mean when you know I *must* have you?

ABSOLUTE: *(Rising)* Nay madam, I shall not support any enforcement on your affection. I promise you, if I have lost your heart then I resign the rest.

LYDIA: *(Rising)* Then, sir, let me tell you, any affection I had for you was acquired by a mean, unmanly deception, and deserves the punishment of fraud. What! You have been treating *me* like a *child!* Humouring my romance, and laughing, I suppose, at your success!

ABSOLUTE: You wrong me Lydia, you wrong me. Only hear –

LYDIA: *(Walking about angrily)* So while *I* flattered myself that I should outwit and enrage my relations. Behold! My hopes are to be crushed at once by my aunt's consent and acceptance! And *I* myself am the only one who is fooled. *(Taking a miniature from her bosom)* But here, sir, here is the picture – *Beverley's* picture which I have worn, night and day, in spite of threats and demands! There, sir *(flings it at him)*, and be assured I throw the original from my heart as easily!

ABSOLUTE: Nay, nay ma'am, we will not disagree on that. *(taking out a picture)* Here is Miss Lydia Languish. What a difference! Aye, *there*

63

is the heavenly, encouraging smile that first touched my soul and raised my hopes! Those are the lips that sealed a vow, such a short time ago. And there the half resentful blush that *would* have curbed the intensity of my advances. Well, all that is past! All over indeed! There, madam – in beauty that copy is not equal to you, but in my mind has more merit than the original since it has not changed. As such, I cannot find it in my heart to part with it. *(Puts it back where he pulled it from)*.

LYDIA: *(Softening)* It is your own doing sir, I – I – I suppose you are perfectly satisfied.

ABSOLUTE: Oh most certainly – for sure now this is much better than being in love! So what if we break so many solemn promises – that does not matter in the least you know. To be sure, people will say that Miss Languish does not know her own mind – but never mind that. Or they may be ill-natured enough to hint that the gentleman grew tired of the lady and abandoned her. But don't let that fret you.

LYDIA: There's no bearing his insolence.

(Bursts into tears. Enter MRS MALAPROP and SIR ANTHONY)

MRS MALAPROP: Come, we must interrupt your billing and cooing for a while.

LYDIA: *(Sobbing)* This is worse than your treachery and deceit, you cad.

SIR ANTHONY: What the devil's the matter now! Zounds! Mrs Malaprop, this is the oddest *billing* and *cooing* I ever heard! What the deuce is the meaning of it? I'm quite astonished!

ABSOLUTE: Ask the lady sir.

MRS MALAPROP: O mercy, I am admonished at you! What is the meaning of this, Lydia?

LYDIA: Ask the gentleman, ma'am.

SIR ANTHONY: Zounds! I shall be in a frenzy! Why, Jack, you have not come out as anyone else have you?

MRS MALAPROP: Aye sir, there's no more tricks are there? You are not three gentlemen at once, are you?

ABSOLUTE: I say the lady can account for this much better than I can.

LYDIA: Ma'am, you once commanded me never to think of Beverley again. There is the man – I now obey you. For, from this moment, I renounce him forever.

(Exit LYDIA)

MRS MALAPROP: O mercy and miracles! What a turnabout this is. Why Captain, you haven't behaved disrespectfully to my niece?

SIR ANTHONY: Ha ha ha! Now I see it. You have been too lively with your first kiss, eh Jack.

ABSOLUTE: Nay, sir, upon my word –

SIR ANTHONY: Come, no lying Jack. You rogue. Ha ha ha poor Lydia.

ABSOLUTE: By all that's good sir –

SIR ATHONY: Zounds! Say no more. I tell you. Mrs Malaprop, you must tell her he was too eager, it is just his way. It runs in the family! Come away, Jack, ha ha ha!

MRS MALAPROP: Oh, Sir Anthony. Captain, you are unbelievable!

(They all leave separately)

Scene 3

(The park. Enter SIR LUCIOUS)

SIR LUCIOUS: I wonder where this captain Absolute hides himself. As an Irishman in this country, I need to be clever. It cannot be thought that I initiated the duel, but instead that it was in self-defence. Then when the deed is done, I shall not be thrown into gaol. Hah! Isn't this the captain coming? He looks much too full of himself, which is mighty provoking. Who the devil is he talking to? (*Steps aside*)

(Enter CAPTAIN ABSOLUTE)

ABSOLUTE: Why did I bother with all my plotting! A noble reward for all my schemes. I did not think her romantic whims could have made her so damned absurd. S'death! I never was in a worse humour in my life! I could cut my own throat, or any other person's with the greatest pleasure.

SIR LUCIOUS: Oh faith! I am in luck. I never could have found him in a sweeter temper for my purpose. Now to enter into a quarrel genteelly. *(SIR LUCIOUS goes up to ABSOLUTE)*. With regard to that matter Captain, I must beg leave to differ in opinion with you.

ABSOLUTE: Upon my word then, you must be a very subtle quarreller, because sir, I happened just then to be giving no opinion at all.

SIR LUCIOUS: That's no excuse. May I tell you a man may *think* an untruth as well as *speak* one.

ABSOLUTE: Very true, sir. But if the man never utters his thoughts, I should think they might stand a chance of escaping controversy.

SIR LUCIOUS: Then, sir, you differ in opinion to me, which amounts to the same thing.

ABSOLUTE: I know who you are Sir Lucious, and if I had not known before that you were a gentleman, upon my soul I would not have known it from this discussion. I cannot conceive what you are driving at unless you mean to quarrel with me!

SIR LUCIOUS: *(Bowing)* I humbly thank you sir, for the quickness of your understanding. You have named the very thing I am at.

ABSOLUTE: Very good sir, and I shall certainly not refuse your wishes. But I should be very pleased if you would explain your motives.

SIR LUCIOUS: Let's finish there sir. The quarrel is a very pretty quarrel as it stands. We should only spoil it by trying to explain it. But let it be known that for the sake of this quarrel, you sir, have proved yourself to be a low, deceitful and cowardly cad.

ABSOLUTE: Do you intend to egg me on into a challenge Sir Lucious? The afront I have given you, whatever it is, surely cannot be so considerable that it demands a challenge.

SIR LUCIOUS: It *demands a challenge* you say. If that is your wish sir, then I accept your demand for a challenge.

ABSOLUTE: My challenge! Zounds sir! You have caught me at the wrong time for your insults and nonsense. At any other time, I should have reasoned this out with you, but in my current disposition, since you seem to be so bent on it, name your time and place. Here and now if you wish!

SIR LUCIOUS: We need a place where we may fight in peace without disruption. We shall meet in Kingsmead fields over yonder, as a little business will call me there at six o'clock, so I may resolve both matters at once.

ABSOLUTE: It is the same for me exactly. A little after six then, and we will discuss this matter more seriously, whatever the matter is!

SIR LUCIOUS: If you please sir, at that time of the challenge, for which *you* have made on me, it will be light enough for a fencing sword but too dark for a long shot.

ABSOLUTE: Agreed.

SIR LUCIOUS: So, the matter's settled, and my mind is at ease.

(Exit SIR LUCIOUS. Enter FAULKLAND)

ABSOLUTE: There's luck, I was about to look for you. O Faulkland, all the demons of spite and disappointment have conspired against me. I'm so disheartened, that if I hadn't the prospect of a challenge ahead, I would not have the spirits to tell you the cause.

FAULKLAND: What can you mean? Has Lydia changed her mind? I should have thought that her duty and her inclination would point to the same person.

ABSOLUTE: Aye, just like the eyes of a person who squints, when her love eye was fixed on me, the other eye, her eye of duty was looking away. But when duty pointed that eye the right way at me, her love eye turned on a swivel and secured its retreat with a frown!

FAULKLAND: Unbelievable! But you mentioned a challenge?

ABSOLUTE: Oh yes, to add to the whole mess, a good-natured Irishman begged leave to have the pleasure of cutting my throat. Or I begged leave of him – I am not too sure. But I mean to indulge him. And there it is!

FAULKLAND: Please be serious!

ABSOLUTE: It is a fact upon my soul. Sir Lucious O'Trigger – you know him by sight – for some affront, which I am sure I never intended, has obliged me to meet him this evening at six o'clock. You must go with me.

FAULKLAND: Nay there must be some mistake. Sir Lucious shall explain himself – and I dare say matters can be resolved. But this evening did you say? I wish it had been any other time.

ABSOLUTE: Why? It will be light enough at 6.

FAULKLAND: I am a good deal ruffled myself because of an argument I had with Julia. My vile temper made me treat her so cruelly, that I shall not be myself until we are reconciled.

ABSOLUTE: By heavens, Faulkland. You don't deserve her.

FAULKLAND: Oh Jack, I have this letter from Julia. I dread to open it. I fear it may be the end. Oh, how I suffer for my folly!

ABSOLUTE: Here, let me see. *(Takes the letter and opens it)* Aye, a final sentence indeed – it is all over with you, faith!

FAULKLAND: Nay Jack. Don't keep me in suspense.

ABSOLUTE: Alright. *As I am convinced that my dear Faulkland's own reflections have already chastised him for his last unkindness to me, I will not add a word on the subject. Meet me in the Tea Rooms at 5 o'clock. Yours ever and truly, Julia.* There's stubbornness and resentment for you! *(Gives him the letter)* Why man, you don't seem one jot happier with this.

FAULKLAND: Oh yes, I am – but – but –

ABSLUTE: Confound your *buts!* You hear something that would make another man bless himself and you immediately damn it with a *but.*

FAULKLAND: Now, Jack, as you are my friend, tell me honestly. Don't you think there is something forward in this haste to forgive? Women should never ask for reconciliation; that should always come from us.

ABSOLUTE: I do not have patience to listen to you. You are incorrigible. Say no more on the subject. Meet me before six on the fields. A poor industrious devil like me, who has toiled and plotted to gain my ends, am now disappointed by other people's folly. But you, a fault-finding, sceptic in love, who has no difficulties apart from those of his own making, is a subject more fitting for ridicule than compassion!

(Exit ABSOLUTE)

FAULKLAND: I feel his reproaches! But I would not change my own disposition for the unruly way *he* tramples on the thorns of love. But his engaging in this duel has given me an idea. I'll use it as a test of Julia's sincerity. If her love proves to be pure then I shall unreservedly give my love forever. But if I see selfishness then it will be best to leave her as a toy for some less cautious fool. *(Exit FAULKLAND)*

Act 5

Scene 1

(Tea rooms. JULIA alone)

JULIA: *(Reading a letter)* How this message has alarmed me! What dreadful situation can he mean? Oh Faulkland, how many unhappy moments and tears have you cost me!

(Enter FAULKLAND)

JULIA: What does this mean Faulkland?

FAULKLAND: Alas Julia, I have come to bid you a long farewell.

JULIA: Heavens! What do you mean?

FAULKLAND: You see before you a wretch, whose life is forfeited. Don't be shocked. My temper has drawn all this misery on me. I left you fretful and passionate – an unexpected accident drew me into a quarrel. The result is that I am due to fight an expert marksman this evening after 6 o'clock. O Julia, had I been so fortunate as to have called you mine, before this misfortune had fallen on me, I should not so deeply dread the ending of my days!

JULIA: My soul is full of sorrow. But I can now chase from your heart every doubt of the warm sincerity of my love. Let us fly from this place together. I know your honour means we may then forfeit our current existence. However, when safe from pursuit, my father's will may be fulfilled, and we shall marry. Then together may we spend our lives, at last, in blissful love.

FAULKLAND: Oh Julia, I am so full of gratitude. But would you not wish some hours to weigh the advantages you forego? For if I abscond then I will be labelled a coward and ostracised from society. I will be left with nothing but my love for you.

JULIA: I do not need a moment. No, Faulkland I have always loved you for yourself. Deserting with you now leaves no room for an attack on my sincerity. But we should not linger. The little I have will be sufficient to support us; and exile should never be splendid.

FAULKLAND: Aye, but in such a degraded state of life, my wounded pride may increase the fretfulness of my temper. Perhaps my past may haunt me in gloomy fits that I shall hate the tenderness you offer me.

JULIA: If you should become so unhappy, you will all the more want an affectionate spirit to console you. One who, with gentleness, may teach you to bear the evils of your misfortune.

FAULKLAND: Julia, you have proven yourself deeply! This was a test of your love and with this device I now throw away all my doubts. I plead only for forgiveness for this last unworthy effect of my restless, unsatisfied disposition.

JULIA: I do not understand. Has there been no challenge as you have told me?

FAULKLAND: I am ashamed to admit that it was all a pretence. Yet in pity, Julia, do not wound me by resenting a fault that will never be repeated. Instead accept my pardon. Let me surrender my years of past folly and look forward to years of tender adoration.

JULIA: Wait, Faulkland! I sincerely rejoice that you have not been called out. But your cruel doubts have put such agony in my heart. It has wounded me more I can express.

FAILKLAND: But Julia....

JULIA: My father loved you, and in his presence I joyfully pledged my hand. When soon after I lost that parent, it seemed to me that providence had, in Faulkland, shown me where to transfer my grateful duty, as well as my affection. Hence, I have been content to bear from you all of the misery caused by your fretfulness and doubts.

FAULKLAND: I confess it all – but hear –

JULIA: No Faulkland! After such a year of trials – I might have flattered myself that I should not have been insulted with a new test of my sincerity. I now see it is not in your nature to be content in love. With this conviction – I never will be yours. I had hopes that my kindness might in time reform your temper. But I will not furnish you with a licenced power to keep alive an incorrigible fault at my expense.

FAULKLAND: But Julia, by my soul and honour, if after this –

JULIA: I shall pray for your happiness with the truest sincerity. I ask Heaven to save you from your unhappy temper, which alone has prevented our solemn engagement. All I request of *you* is that when you count up the many true delights it has deprived you of, let it not be your *least* regret that it lost you the love of one who would have followed you in beggary through the world!

(Exit JULIA via upstairs room door)

FAULKLAND: She's gone. There was an awful resolution in her manner that riveted me in place. O fool – barbarian, cursed that I am! Kind fortune sent a heaven gifted cherub to my aid, and I have driven her from my side! I must now haste to my appointment. Well, my mind is set for such a scene. O Love! Tormentor, whose influence makes idiots of men and urges sense into madness! I only wish that I would become an active participant in a duel as I pretended to my Julia. Then I would surely receive all I deserved.

(Exit FAULKAND. Enter LYDIA)

LYDIA: Hey-ho! Though he has used me so badly, this fellow runs strangely in my head. I believe one lecture from my serious cousin will make me recall him.

(Re-enter JULIA)

LYDIA: O Julia, I have come to you with such an appetite to be consoled. Lud! Julia, what's the matter with you? You have been crying. I'll be hanged if that Faulkland has not been tormenting you!

JULIA: You are mistaken – something has flurried me a little – but nothing you can guess at. *(Aside)* I would not accuse Faulkland to a sister!

LYDIA: Ah whatever troubles you may have, I can assure you mine surpass them. You would not guess who Beverley proves to be!

JULIA: I will now confess, Lydia, that Mr Faulkland had before informed me of the whole affair. Had young Absolute truly been an ensign, I should not have accepted your confidence without a serious endeavour to change your mind.

LYDIA: So, then I see I have been deceived by everyone! But I don't care – I'll never have him.

JULIA: Nay, Lydia –

LYDIA: It is so provoking. I thought we were heading for an exciting life of hardship. I had planned a most sentimental elopement. Wearing a cunning disguise, shinning down a ladder of ropes, a beautiful moon, four horses, a sympathetic parson, with such a surprise to Mrs Malaprop, and such paragraphs in the newspapers! Oh, I shall die with disappointment!

JULIA: I don't wonder.

LYDIA: Now – a sad reverse. What have I to expect but, after a deal of tedious preparation with a bishop's licence, and my aunt's blessing, to go simpering up to the alter, with the consent of every butcher in the parish.

JULIA: Melancholy indeed!

LYDIA: How mortifying, to remember the delicious encounters we arranged to gain half a minute's conversation! How often have I stole out in the coldest night in January, and found him in the garden, stuck like a dripping statue. There he would kneel in the snow and sneeze and cough so pathetically! He shivering with cold and I with apprehension! And while the freezing wind numbed our joints, how warmly we would glow with mutual passion! Ah Julia, that was something like being in love.

JULIA: If I were in spirits Lydia, I should chide you only by laughing at you. But my disposition instead bids me to entreat you not to let a man, who loves you with sincerity, suffer that unhappiness from your fickleness that I know it can inflict.

LYDIA: *(Voices outside)* O Lud! What brought my aunt here!

(Enter MRS MALAPROP, LUCY, FAG and DAVID)

73

MRS MALAPROP: So, so! Here's fine work! There's assassination, extermination, annihilation, palpitation and constipation going on in the fields and Sir Anthony not to be found to prevent this apostrophe.

JULIA: For heaven's sake madam, what's the meaning of this?

MRs MALAPROP: That gentleman can tell you. He concealed the whole affair to me.

LYDIA: *(To FAG)* Sir, do please inform us.

FAG: Ma'am, I should hold myself very deficient as a man of breeding, if I delayed a moment to give all the information in my power to a lady so deeply interested in the affair as you are.

LYDIA: Be quick! Quick sir!

FAG: True ma'am, as you say, one should be quick in divulging matters of this nature; for should we be tedious, perhaps while we are dwelling on the subject, two or three lives may be lost!

LYDIA: O patience! Do ma'am for heaven's sake tell us what is the matter?

MRS MALAPROP: Why murder's the matter! Slaughter's the matter! Killings the matter! But he can tell you the perpendiculars.

LYDIA: Then please sir, be brief!

FAG: Why then as to murder – I cannot really say myself. As to slaughter, or manslaughter, that will be as the jury finds it.

LYDIA: But who sir – who are engaged in this.

FAG: Faith, ma'am, one is a young gentleman whom I should be very sorry anything was to happen to – a very well-behaved gentleman! We have lived much together and always on good terms.

LYDIA: But who is this? Who! Who! Who! *(Picking up a fork from the table).* The next word you speak will be the name of a person or murder may come sooner than you think!

FAG: My master ma'am – my master – I speak of my master.

LYDIA: Heavens! What, Captain Absolute?

MRS MALAPROP: Oh to be sure, you are frightened now!

JULIA: But who are with him sir?

FAG: As to the rest ma'am, this gentleman can inform you better than I.

JULIA: *(To DAVID)* Do speak, friend.

DAVID: Lookee my lady – by the heavens! There's mischief going on – folks don't meet for amusement with firearms, firelocks, fire-engines, fire officers and the devil knows what other crackers besides! This, my lady, has an angry appearance!

JULIA: But who is there beside Captain Absolute, friend?

DAVID: My poor master. You know me lady – I am David – and my latest master is, or *was* if we are too late, Squire Acres. Then there is also Squire Faulkland.

JULIA: Faulkland! Do ma'am let us go instantly in order to prevent mischief.

MRS MALAPROP: Oh fie – it would be very inelegant of us. We would only aggregate things.

DAVID: Ah do! Mrs Aunt, save a few lives – they are desperately driven, believe me. Above all there is that bloodthirsty philistine, Sir Lucious O'Trigger.

MRS MALAPROP: Sir Lucious O'Trigger! O mercy! Have they drawn poor little dear Sir Lucious into the fight?

LUCY: *(In clever voice)* O heavens, what cantankerous altercation is coalescing with our poor Irishman!

(They all look at her in amazement)

(In simpleton voice) I means O Lud, guvnor, what an awful thingamabob to 'appen.

LYDIA: What are we to do madam?

MRS MALAPROP: Why fly with the utmost viscosity to be sure to prevent mischief. Friend – can you show us to the place?

FAG: If you please ma'am I will lead you. David, look for Sir Anthony.

DAVD: Yes, Mr Fag.

(Exit DAVID)

MRS MALAPROP: Come girls, this gentleman will exhort us. Come, sir, lead the way and we'll precede. You're sure you know the spot.

FAG: I think I can find it ma'am. With luck we shall hear the pistols as we draw near, so we can't miss them. Never fear ma'am, never fear!

Scene 2

(In the park. SIR ANTHONY out for a stroll. Enter DAVID Running)

DAVID: O Sir Anthony! Murder! Thief! Fire! Stop!

SIR ANTHONY: Fire! Murder! Where?

DAVID: Aye, please you, Sir Anthony, there's all kinds of murder. All sorts of slaughter to be seen in the fields. There's fighting going on, sir. Bloody sword and gun fighting!

SIR ANTHONY: Who are going to fight dunce?

DAVID: Everybody that I know of Sir Anthony. Everybody! Mr Acres, Sir Lucious O'Trigger, your son the Captain –

SIR ANTHONY: What! Oh, the dog! What's he up to now! Do you know the place?

DAVID: Kingsmead Fields over yonder.

SIR ANTHONY: Run and get assistance and bring them to the place. I'll put a stop to this nonsense directly!

(SIR ANTHONY stomps off. DAVID turns and runs into FAULKLAND)

DAVID: Oh sir, I am so pleased it is you. Have they stopped the murder and madness?

FAULKLAND: No David, the madness continues and I am on my way there now as I have promised to my friend.

DAVID: Oh, sir we must get assistance and go to the Fields urgently. Come, come! Fire! Murder!

FAULKLAND: Hold there David. Do not be concerned. The honourable affair cannot start without me. There is a related matter that I must discuss with you, and it cannot wait. David, my happiness, my future and that of another is entirely in your hands.

DAVID: My hands sir? If I can be of any assistance I will, but I trust it is something we can resolve quickly. We should go to Kingsmead Fields directly.

FAULKLAND: That is what I want you to do David. Come to the fields quickly with me, wearing this hooded cloak so you cannot be recognised.

DAVID: By heavens sir, why should you want me to play masquerades at a time like this!

FAULKLAND: I will go straight to the heart of the matter for you David. You and I are to have a duel at the fields after the others are done.

DAVID: What! Zounds sir! This is not the time for jesting! And such a poor taste of jest to be sure!

FAULKAND: It is no jest. Here is your pistol!

DAVID: My pistol! Zounds! I would never even touch one of those bloody-minded weapons let alone use it against a gentleman such as you. Here am I trying to stop the challenges while at the same time you are trying to add to them! Why sir do you wish to shoot this poor servant. If it is for honour sir, then I gladly hand over all my honour and valour without the need for blowing my head off. Why, sir, I have a new hat and I need a place to set it on.

FAULKLAND. Nay nay, David, do be easy. I have no quarrel with you. The whole affair between us is a masquerade. Both pistols have powder without shot. We shall face each other and agree to shoot in the air as honourable gentlemen should. We shall shake hands and leave.

DAVID: Oh, by heavens! So poor David will not be killed this day. I am forever grateful sir. But pray tell me why we are engaging in this sham-fight with the air?

FAULKLAND: I trust by this act, that I can reclaim the affections of the lady whom I have treated excessively badly. When she hears that I indeed did face a challenge and survived, I hold great hopes that we can be reconciled, and at last fulfil her father's wishes.

DAVID: Then sir, if it is for love, and I can support your endeavours, and since you have promised to keep my head attached to my shoulders for the sake of my new hat, I shall be pleased to provide assistance in this masquerade.

FAULKLAND: David, I am indeed truly grateful to you. Now. Let us make haste while I tell you how the masquerade will work.

(They leave quickly)

Scene 3

(Kingsmead Fields. SIR LUCIOUS and ACRES with pistols.)

ACRES: By my valour! Sir Lucious, forty yards is a good distance. Odds. Levels and aims, I say a good distance.

SIR LUCIOUS: Is this for muskets or field cannon? Upon my conscience Mr Acres, you must leave these things to me. Stay now, I'll show you. *(Measures a few steps along the stage)* There now, that is a very pretty distance – a pretty gentleman's distance.

ACRES: Zounds! We might as well fight in a sentry box! I tell you, Sir Lucious, the farther he is off, the cooler I shall take aim.

SIR LUCIOUS: Faith! Then I suppose you would aim at him best of all if he was out of sight!

ACRES: No, Sir Lucious – but I should think forty, or eight and thirty yards.

SIR LUCIOUS: Pho, pho! Nonsense! Three or four feet between the mouths of your pistols is as good as a mile.

ACRES: Odds, bullets, no! By my valour, there is no merit in killing him so near. I can see my new coat becoming a mess. Do my dear Sir Lucious let me bring him down at a long shot!

SIR LUCIOUS: Well, the gentleman's friend and I must settle that. But tell me now, Mr Acres, in case of accident, is there any little will or commission I could execute for you?

ACRES: I am much obliged to you, Sir Lucious, but I don't understand.

SIR LUCIOUS: Why, there's no being shot at without a little risk. If an unlucky bullet should carry a quietus with it – a deadly wound - I say that would not be the time to be bothering you about family matters.

ACRES: Quietus!

SIR LUCIOUS: For instance, if that should be the case, would you choose to be pickled and sent home, or would it be all the same to you to lie here in the Abbey? I'm told it is very snug lying in the Abbey.

ACRES: Pickled? Snug lying in the Abbey! Odds, tremors Sir Lucious! Don't talk so!

SIR LUCIOUS: I suppose Mr Acres, you never were engaged in an affair of this kind before?

ACRES: No, Sir Lucious, never before.

SIR LUCIOUS: Ah that's a pity! There's nothing like being used to a thing. Pray now, how will you receive the gentleman's shot?

ACRES: Odds, narrows and files! I've practised that. *(Turns himself sidewards and strikes a shooting attitude)* There, Sir Luscious – there. A side-front hey! Odds, I'll make myself small enough – I'll stand edge ways.

SIR LUCIOUS: Nay sir. If you stand that way when I take my aim *(levelling at him) –*

ACRES: Woooah Sir Lucious! Are you sure it is not cocked?

SIR LUCIOUS: Never fear.

ACRES: But, but, you know it may go off on its own.

SIR LUCIOUS: Pho! Be easy. Well now, if I hit you in the body, my bullet has a double chance. For if it misses a vital part on your right side then it will be hard for it not to succeed on the left.

ACRES: A vital part!

SIR LUCIOUS: But here – stand like this *(Placing him face on)*. Let him see the broadside of your full front – there – now a ball or two may pass clean through your body, and never do any harm at all.

ACRES: Clean through me! A ball or two clean through me!

SIR LUCIOUS: Aye, and besides it is a far more gentlemanly stance.

ACRES: Lookee! Sir Lucious! I'd prefer to be shot in an awkward posture as a gentlemanly one. *(Pulling in his stomach)* I will stand edge ways.

SIR LUCIOUS: *(Looking at his watch)* Surely they don't mean to disappoint us. Hah! No faith – I see them coming.

ACRES: Hey! What! Coming?

SIR LUCIOUS: Aye, who are those getting over the stile?

ACRES: There are two of them, indeed! Well, let them come, hey sir Lucious! We – we – we – we won't run –

SIR LUCIOUS: Run!

ACRES: No – I say – we *won't* run, by my valour.

SIR LUCIOUS: What the devil's the matter with you?

ACRES: Nothing – nothing – my dear friend – my dear Sir Lucious – but I – I – I don't feel quite so bold, somehow – as I did.

SIR LUCIOUS: O fie! Consider your honour.

ACRES: Aye – true – my honour – do, Sir Lucious, put in a word or two every now and again about my honour.

SIR LUCIOUS: *(Looking)* Well, here they are coming. Yet who is that creature in a hooded robe following some way behind?

ACRES: A hooded figure? Zounds! It is not the ghost of death is it? Sir Lucious. If I wasn't with you, I should almost think I was afraid that my valour should leave me! Valour will come and go.

SIR LUCIOUS: Then pray keep it now while you have it.

ACRES: Sir Lucious. I feel it is going. Yes my valour is certainly going! It is sneaking off! I feel it oozing out as if it were on the palms of my hands.

SIR LUCIOUS: Your honour, man, your honour! Hark, the leading two are here.

ACRES: Oh mercy! Now? I wish I were safe in my manor or could be shot before I was aware!

(ABSOLUTE and FAULKLAND enter to the side and stop. SIR LUCIOUS practises with ACRES)

ABSOLUTE: Faulkland, I cannot believe you can be so ridiculous! So that hooded numskull who has been following us is David and you intend to have a duel with him!

FAULKLAND: Only a pretend duel, Jack. A pretend duel. It is the only way I see to reclaim my Julia. You'll help me, will you?

ABSOLUTE: I will, I will. This is a pretty mess. Heavens only knows how this day will end. Come now, we are here.

(Enter FAULKLAND and ABSOLUTE)

SIR LUCIOUS: Gentlemen, your most obedient – Hah! Captain Absolute! So, I suppose sir you have come here, just like myself, to do a kind of office, first for your friend, then proceed to business on your own account.

ACRES: What Jack! My dear Jack! My dear friend!

ABSOLUTE: Harkee, Bob, Beverley's at hand.

SIR LUCIOUS: *(To FAULKLAND)* So, Mr Beverley, if you'll chose your weapons, the Captain and I will measure the ground.

FAULKLAND: *My* weapons, sir

ACRES: Odds life! Sir Lucious. I'm not going to fight Mr Faulkland. These are my particular friends.

SIR LUCIOUS: What sir, did you not come here to fight Mr Acres?

FAULKLAND: Not I, upon my word sir,

SIR LUCIOUS: Well, now, that is mighty provoking! But I hope, Mr Faulkland, as there are three of us who have come here for the game, you won't be so cantankerous as to spoil the party by sitting out.

ABSOLUTE: O pray, Faulkland, fight to oblige Sir Lucious.

FAULKLAND: Nay, if Mr Acres is so bent on the matter.

ACRES: No, no, Mr Faulkland. I'll bear my disappointment like a Christian. Lookee Sir Lucious, there's no reason at all for me to fight, and if it is all the same to you, I'd better let it alone.

SIR LUCIOUS: Harkee Mr Acres. I must not be trifled with. You have certainly challenged somebody, and you came her to fight him. Now, if the gentleman is willing to represent him, I can't see why it isn't just the same thing.

ACRES: Why no, Sir Lucious, I tell you it is one Beverley I've challenged. A fellow, you see, that dare not show his face! If he were here, I'd make him give up his claims directly!

SIR LUCIOUS: That hooded man yonder. Perhaps he is this Beverley, sneaking about by the trees.

ACRES: Nay, nay, not that ghostly dark apparition. That cannot be Beverley! Sir Lucious, remind me of my honour, my honour!

FAULKLAND: Steady Mr Acres. That gentleman has an argument with me. It shall be resolved soon enough.

SIR LUCIOUS: So, sir, you *have* come to play the game.

FAULKLAND: Indeed so sir, but with that mysterious gentleman alone.

ABSOLUTE: Hold Bob, let me set you right. There is no such man as Beverley. The person who assumed that name is standing before you. As his claims to the lady are the same in both characters, he is ready to support them in any way you please.

SIR LUCIOUS: Well, this is lucky. Now you have an opportunity –

ACRES: What! Quarrel with my dear friend Jack Absolute! Not if he were fifty Beverley's. Zounds! Sir Lucious, you will not make me.

SIR LUCIOUS: Upon my conscience, Mr Acres, your valour has *oozed* away with a vengeance!

ACRES: Not in the least! Odds, backs and abettors. I'll be your second with all my heart. And if you get a *quietus*, you may command me entirely. I'll get you a snug lying in the Abbey here, or *pickle* you, and send you back to Blunderbuss Hall.

SIR LUCIOUS: Pho, pho! You are little better than a coward.

ACRES: Mind gentlemen, he calls me a *coward*. Coward was the word, by my valour!

SIR LUCIOUS: Well, sir?

ACRES: Lookee Sir Lucious. It isn't that I mind the word coward – *coward* may be said in joke. But if you had called me a *poltroon*, odds, daggers and balls!

SIR LUCIOUS: Well sir?

ACRES: I should have thought you a very ill-bred man.

SIR LUCIOUS: Pho, you are beneath my notice.

ABSOLUTE: Nay, Sir Lucious, you can't have a better second than my friend, Acres. He is a most *determined dog* – called in the country, '*Fighting Bob*', eh?

ACRES: Nay nay. I said *Reciting* Bob on account of my love of poetry.

SIR LUCIOUS: Well, then Captain, we must begin – so come out, my little counsellor *(draws his sword)* and ask the gentleman whether he will resign without forcing you to proceed against him?

ABSOLUTE: Come then sir *(Draws)*. Since you won't be amicable, here's my reply.

(Enter SIR ANTHONY and the WOMEN)

SIR ANTHONY: Put up Jack, put up or I shall be in a frenzy. Why are you in a duel, sir?

ABSOLUTE: Faith sir, that gentleman can tell you better than I. It was he who challenged me without explaining his reasons.

SIR ANTHONY: Gad sir, why did you call my son out without explaining your reasons.

SIR LUCIOUS: Nay sir, it was your son who called me out. He most decidedly said it *demands a challenge*. Those were his very words.

SIR ANTHONY: Zounds Jack. Do you deny those words?

ABSOLUTE: Those words were indeed spoken, but I am unsure whose head created them.

MRS MALAPROP: How can such a small group of men create such great contusion in just one day! Come, come, let's have no challenges before ladies. Captain Absolute, how can you frighten us so. Lydia has been verified to death for you.

ABSOLUTE: For fear I should be killed or escape ma'am?

MRS MALAPROP: Nay, no delusions to the past. Lydia is convinced. Speak child. *(Lydia remains shyly silent)*

SIR LUCIOUS. By your leave ma'am, I must put in a word here. I believe I can interpret the lady's silence. Now –

LYDIA: What do you mean sir?

SIR LUCIOUS: Come, come my dear Delia, we must be serious now. This is no time for jesting.

LYDIA: I have no interest in jesting sir. Why do you address a complete stranger so affectionately under an assumed name. There is only one man here who has my full heart, and it is not you sir.

SIR LUCIOUS: Come, come. We are not strangers! You do not need to hide our deep affection now from those around you. It is time for us to reveal ourselves. Do you deny your own handwriting here *(Takes out letters)*

MRS MALAPROP: *(Aside)* Oh he will dissolve my mystery! - Sir Lucious, I believe there is some mistake. Perhaps I can provide some resistance.

SIR LUCIOUS: Pray, old gentlewoman, don't interfere where you have no business. Miss Languish, are you my Delia or are you not?

LYDIA: Indeed, Sir Lucious, I am not.

SIR LUCIOUS: You are not! What mischief is afoot here?

MRS MALAPROP. Sir Lucious O'Trigger – ungrateful as you are – pardon my blushes. I am Delia.

SIR LUCIOUS: You Delia? Pho! Be easy!

MRS MALAPROP: Why thou barbarous Vandyke. Those letters are mine. When you are more appreciable of my kindness and defection, perhaps I may be convinced to continue to respond to your fallacious correspondence.

SIR LUCIOUS: Zounds! This comes as a mighty surprise. I am cut to the bone. Captain Absolute, it appears I am mistaken and have no claim on the Lady Lydia. My apologies. Give me your hand, and we shall call it settled.

ABSOLUTE: Indeed sir. I am pleased to say it is settled.

SIR LUCIOUS: I am much obliged. You are indeed an honourable man. Now, since I have been disappointed myself, it would give me great satisfaction to see other people succeed better. My Lady Lydia. I apologise for my earlier advances. You said before there is but one man who has your heart. It would be a fine consolation for me to see you resolve that connection with a gentleman as gallant as Captain Absolute.

CAPTAIN ABSOLUTE: Oh, my little angel. Dare I implore you to forgive my faults and failures.

LYDIA: Indeed sir, should you wish to reassert your previous entreaties, I can confidently assure you of a very different style of response.

SIR ANTHONY: At last, some sense and finality. I suggest we move earnestly to the marriage date before any one of you changes your mind, or your person, again.

SIR LUCIOUS: Mrs Malaprop. Whether you or Lucy put this trick on me, I am equally beholden to you. And to show I am not ungrateful, Captain Absolute. Since you have taken that lady from me, I'll give you my Delia into the bargain.

ABSOLUTE: I am much obliged to you, Sir Lucious, but here's our friend Fighting Bob unprovided for.

ACRES: Odds, wrinkles! No. But give me your hand Sir Lucious. Forget and forgive. If ever I give you the chance of pickling me again, say Bob Acres is a dunce, that's all.

SIR ANTHONY: Come, Mrs Malaprop, don't be cast down. You are in your bloom yet.

MRS MALAPROP: O Sir Anthony! Men are all Bavarians! *(She stomps off)*

SIR LUSCIOUS: *(To LUCY).* Now vixen, you owe me three crowns, two gold pocket charms and a silver snuff box!

LUCY: *(Serious voice)* Oh sir, but they are sold and invested already, and now sit happily within my expanding fortune. *(Simpleton voice)* But you still owes me fifty kisses m'lud, unless your modesty don't allow 'em.

SIR LUSCIOUS: Modesty be damned. It is a debt I shall happily accept. And here is a downpayment. *(Kisses her)*

FALKLAND: Gentlemen and ladies, I am very pleased for you all, but now I must conclude my own business with the eerie gentleman standing over yonder.

ACRES: Odds, phantoms and goosebumps. Is the apparition still there? He drains me of what is left of my valour just by his very appearance!

ABSOLUTE: He comes. *(DAVID steps into position for the duel)*

SIR LUCIOUS: I am at a loose end. I shall offer my services as second to this strange adversary. *(DAVID draws near still with his face hidden. SIR LUCIOUS meets him)*

JULIA: But what is this Faulkland? You told me your challenge was all a pretence!

FAULKLAND: Do not be afraid Julia. I did not wish to vex you – but the pretence of a pretence was a pretence. It is an appointment that I must keep. If I do not return, please know that my deep affection for you is, and has always been, real and immovable. *(FAULKLAND prepares for the duel)*

SIR ANTHONY: Egad, this is too much. I shall stop this interaction directly.

ABSOLUTE: Sir, this is such a peculiar type of insult that the challenge cannot be prevented. It is a delicate matter to explain before ladies so I must whisper in your ear the particulars of this case. *(ABSOLUTE whispers to SIR ANTHONY who smiles when he hears the story. ABSOLUTE joins FAULKLAND).*

JULIA: Mr Acres, can you please talk earnestly to my Faulkland and save him from this barbarous act.

ACRES: I am desperately sorry my lady, but I am assured the nature of the challenge can only be resolved in this manner. But if Mr Faulkland fires high, we shall hope this mysterious gentleman behaves honourably.

SIR LUCIOUS: You would not believe it Captain Absolute, but that numbskull had forgotten to load shot in his pistol. As luck would have it, I spotted the error in time and have loaded it for him.

ABSOLUTE: What!

SIR LUCIOUS: This hooded creature seems to have even less valour than Mr Acres. He shakes like an aspen leaf. A rude fellow too – he gave no thanks whatever when I loaded his pistol, yet I suspect it will be the saving of him.

ABSOLUTE: Zounds! I must stop the duel!

SIR LUCIOUS: Too late.

(They raise their pistols. FAULKLAND fires first into the air. DAVID is so shocked that he spins around wildly, firing the pistol in the air but in FAULKLAND's direction. FAULKLAND falls to the ground with slight blood on his temple.)

ALL: *Sounds of shock and dismay*

(JULIA rushes out to FAULKLAND. Others circle at a distance. DAVID throws off his cloak and sinks to his knees. He is comforted by ACRES.

SIR LUCIOUS: There! How fortuitous that I gave him that shot! *(Shouting)* Well done young man!

JULIA: Oh, my poor Faulkland. How can it end so. I wish with all my heart I had not chastised him the way I did. I vow there will be no other man who shall earn my affection. I shall stay a spinster for my entire life as a tribute to the love we once had.

FAULKLAND: *(Groans)*

JULIA: My Faulkland lives. He is back with me! Can you speak, dear Faulkland? *(they all show relief)*

FAULKLAND: Julia. It is but a graze past my head. I shall recover. But I heard what you said, and I now know, even more than ever, that your love for me is completely in earnest. From this moment forwards I shall never doubt you again. *(He stands shakily)*

JULIA: You won't doubt me you say. But you know Faulkland that my love for you is surely based on my father's wishes.

FAULKLAND: Zounds! I am happy for his confidence in me. I would be honoured if Sir Anthony, Captain Absolute and all my friends also commit me to you. Then you dare not leave me!

JULIA: But Faulkland, if it was not for you saving my life from the raging waters, I may not be so enamoured.

FAULKLAND: Then we shall go to the depths of the jungle full of ferocious creatures, to the highest mountains, and to tea with Mrs

Malaprop so that I can save you again and again, such that you are even more indebted to me for the rest of your life.

JULIA: I am so deliriously happy. So happy that I shall go dancing with my cousin Lydia. A raging country jig with spins, leaps and many hand passes with handsome young men while you manage business alone in our manor.

FAULKLAND: Throw Sir Lucious into the bargain and have a most spectacular evening of merriment. Although be prepared for him leaving early on account of his need to challenge anyone who tangles with you.

JULIA: Oh, my Faulkland. We are at last together. But if it is just the shot wound on your head talking, then be it known that I shall strike you with a cudgel once a week for the rest of your life.

(ACRES comes over with DAVID)

ACRES: Come now Fighting David, you have earned yourself a celebration. The masquerade has performed as hoped. *(To everyone)* My dear friends, the whole business is settled, one way or another. Come gentlemen and ladies. Odds, drums and pipes! I'll order the fiddles in half an hour. To the New Rooms so we may all celebrate this extraordinary day.

(They all leave except LUCY)

LUCY: *(Common voice)* There's no place for me in that celebration.

(Clever voice). Yet... It's a common observation that the evils of love are more numerous than its blessings. But I believe that these evils are mostly of our own creating.

When hearts deserving happiness unite, virtue crowns them with an unfading garland of modest hurtless flowers. But when love is based on passion, greed, and mistrust then the garland is made of an ostensibly brighter but gaudier rose whose thorns will grow to offend.

What of our two couples? It was clear that their relationships were thwarted by dishonesty and mistrust, leading them to that offensive gaudy crown. For one, the retreat of the controlling aunt and overbearing father allowed the deep love to blossom from under their repressive shadow to spawn those gentle petals.

For the other it took a muzzle shot to knock sense into the poisonous thoughts of one lover, blasting the thorns away and liberating the affection and trust that had been trapped within.

As for me. My Sir Luscious was too smitten by an illusion to see the flower right under his nose. And though I am not of the right station. (*Common voice*) More of a weed than a rose, once I gets 'old of his money, and makes him a rich man again, he'll blooming well be mine forever and I'll have as many roses as I wants.

So here is my message. For you patriarchs and matriarchs, don't bridle young lovers with your baggage but let them experience their shortfalls and triumphs to find their own destiny. For those who are now left free to follow their hearts, be open, be honest, be happy, be good, be loving, but most of all do not…. behave!

(Exit laughing)